Rose Sheifer & Liz Aneloski

Vintage Tablecloth Quilts

kitchen kitsch to bedroom chic

12 projects to piece or appliqué

C&T PUBLISHING

Text copyright © 2012 by Rose Sheifer and Liz Aneloski

Inspirational Photography copyright © 2012 by Rose Sheifer

Photography and Artwork copyright © 2012 by C&T Publishing, Inc.

Publisher: Amy Marson

Creative Director: Gailen Runge

Art Director: Kristy Zacharias

Editor: Liz Aneloski

Technical Editors: Alison M. Schmidt and Gailen Runge

Cover/Book Designer: April Mostek

Page Layout Artist: Kerry Graham

Production Coordinator: Zinnia Heinzmann

Production Editor: S. Michele Fry

Illustrator: Jessica Jenkins

How-to and style photography by Christina Carty-Francis and Diane Pedersen of C&T Publishing, Inc., unless otherwise noted

Inspirational photography by Rose Sheifer, unless otherwise noted

Published by C&T Publishing, Inc., P.O. Box 1456, Lafayette, CA 94549

Library of Congress Cataloging-in-Publication Data

Sheifer, Rose, 1953-

Vintage tablecloth quilts : kitchen kitsch to bedroom chic - 12 projects to piece or appliqué / Rose Sheifer and Liz Aneloski.

pages cm

ISBN 978-1-60705-469-6 (soft cover)

1. Machine quilting--Patterns. 2. Machine appliqué--Patterns. 3. Tablecloths. I. Aneloski, Liz, 1955- II. Title.

TT835.S4642 2012

746.44'5041--dc23

2012004058

Printed in China

10 9 8 7 6 5 4 3 2 1

Contents

Dedication

From Rose:

To the four most significant people in my life: my wonderful mother, Millie Schiafone; my second mother, Marion Quinn; my very supportive husband, Bruce; and my dear son, Will.

From Liz:

To my husband, Mark. Thank you for three decades of love, laughter, challenges, and support—the things that make life worth living.

Acknowledgments

First and foremost I am eternally grateful for my co-author and longtime colleague, Liz Aneloski. Without her participation this book simply would not be. Thank you so much, Liz. I learned a heck of a lot!

Thank you to my dear friend Sharyn Amoroso…for all the "walk and talks" where you are always my sounding board helping me sort things out.

The encouragement from Dena Fishbein of Dena Designs gave me the confidence to move forward with my idea. Thank you for also providing your gorgeous fabric for the combination quilt (*Dena's Delight*).

Thank you to David and Sandy Ogden for loaning your incredible Bauer pottery pieces that worked so perfectly with the quilts.

I could not have sewn twelve quilts without a place to do it. I am still awestruck by the conversion of my garage into an amazing sewing studio by two very talented individuals, Larry and Brent Russell, the contractors who made it happen.

And last but not least, I am so grateful to everyone at C&T for giving me this opportunity. Special thanks to those incredible photo gals, Diane Pedersen and Christina Carty-Francis, for all the beautiful shots, and for the exquisite design skills of April Mostek.

Thank you also to the following companies for providing us with wonderful fabrics and supplies:

Moda Home	RJR Fabrics
Moda Fabrics	Robert Kaufman Fabrics
P&B Textiles	Timeless Treasures Fabrics
Quilters Dream Batting	Westminster Fibers / FreeSpirit Fabrics

Introduction

By Rose Sheifer

Vintage tablecloths! Most people have at least one (or more) stored away in the back of a linen closet or drawer. Those vibrantly colored, oddly shaped, and slightly stained or torn tablecloths handed down to you by your mother or grandmother are waiting to serve a purpose once again.

My stash of vintage tablecloths consisted of about ten, in a variety of sizes, colors, and patterns. I sometimes used them to cover tables for outdoor parties, set with mismatched vintage plates and vases filled with garden flowers. When not in use, the tablecloths were ironed and folded neatly on a shelf for display. They were too beautiful to be tucked away in the back of the closet.

One day while having coffee surrounded by my gorgeous tablecloths, it came to me: These are amazing works of art! The stains and holes were a problem, but what if I used the pieces of them to build quilts? This was the birth of *Vintage Tablecloth Quilts*. Having designed more than 200 books on quilting and crafts over many years as a graphic designer, I was always looking at the creative work of artists from across the country. Now it was my turn.

As a graphic artist, I have learned to master software programs such as Adobe Photoshop and Illustrator. Using my digital camera and technical skills, I began to create designs with fabric swatches from the Internet. This process allowed me the ease and flexibility to create designs quickly. The finished quilts are almost identical to my original digital designs.

I called on my friend and longtime colleague Liz Aneloski, developmental editor for C&T Publishing, with the hope that she would be my co-author. With her extraordinary technical skills and keen eye for style and color, I felt we could bring this concept to life. Liz carefully reviewed my designs to make sure the recipes would work. Adjustments were made when needed, and in the end twelve unique quilts were made, each using a vintage or reproduction tablecloth as the starting point. Watching these tablecloths take on a new life has been extraordinary. They are now out of the closet!

Section One:
Starting with a Vintage Tablecloth

Vintage Tablecloths

A Little Background Information

If you look into the history of the manufacturing of household textiles beginning in the 1920s, you will inevitably come across the name of Weil and Durrse. The company, run by two brothers in the Garment District of New York City, produced the famous Wilendur brand of tablecloths. What made Wilendur products stand out were the bold, vibrant colors, the shading and highlighting, and the use of gray shadows. They also are recognized by the beautiful artwork, mostly of florals and fruit. These richly colored and exquisitely designed tablecloths became the benchmark for all other manufacturers to follow.

Originally, the tablecloths were printed on imported linen. However, during World War II the linen became difficult to acquire, so the tablecloths were then made of domestic cotton sailcloth, a very durable fabric. As time went on, other fabrics were used, such as cotton blends and synthetics.

Where Can You Find Vintage Tablecloths?

The very first place to look for vintage tablecloths is in your own linen closet or drawers. Many of us have them handed down from our mothers and grandmothers.

If you don't have any, try the following options:

- Flea markets (antique and traditional)
- Antique shops
- Garage sales
- Online auctions (eBay)
- Internet searches
- Etsy
- Moda Home (reproduction vintage tablecloths)

The price range varies based on the condition, popularity, and brand. I have paid as little as $15 and as much as $35. You can pay a lot more if you are willing.

How to Clean Your Tablecloths

To clean your tablecloth, first try rinsing it by hand to remove surface dirt. Let the water run clean and be gentle when wringing, especially with weaker fabrics.

Understand that some stains are never going to come out. Never use bleach because it can easily weaken the old fabric as well as cause discoloration.

I use an OxiClean soak with very hot water in a bucket for a few hours and check to see if the stains have released. If not, I soak for a few more hours or overnight. It may take several tries. You will have to rinse the tablecloth several times to make sure all the detergent is gone.

It's best to dry tablecloths on a clothesline or grass lawn. The sun and fresh air can do wonders for minimizing stains and bringing out the whites.

For more information on specific stains, visit www.vintagetableclothsclub.com/stains.htm.

Press the tablecloth while it is still slightly damp to crisp the fabric. Softer fabrics can benefit from spray starch or Best Press to give them more stability during cutting and sewing.

How to Choose a Tablecloth for Your Quilt

You will need to determine which parts of the tablecloth are usable. Stains can be a challenge, but don't let them deter you; sometimes you can cut around them. They also become less noticeable after the quilt is pieced and quilted. Stay away from very faded and very worn tablecloths because they probably will not hold up to cutting accurately and stitching. It is really a matter of seeing how much fabric is available to use in the final quilt. Loosely woven tablecloths can be stabilized by adding a lightweight fusible interfacing. Just fuse an oversized piece of interfacing to the wrong side before cutting out the motifs.

A tablecloth with a repetitive-design pattern might contain anywhere from four to twelve usable areas. Smaller motifs can be used as accents in alternate blocks. Borders can be made from an overall floral pattern. Combining tablecloths is also an option as the colors and designs from the era tend to complement one another.

Open up the tablecloth and use a measuring tape to see what you actually have before you begin to cut.

Take your needed cutting area into consideration, making sure you have enough fabric to cut all the blocks evenly. We had to unhem one tablecloth to have enough fabric to cut out the block. Using a square cutting ruler the same size as or larger than the cut size will make cutting easier than using a smaller rectangular ruler.

TIPS

- Make a template, using template plastic, the cut size of your motif to use as a pattern to help make sure you will be able to cut the necessary motif sizes from the tablecloth.

- Place masking tape on your square cutting ruler, at the cut-size dimensions, to help you cut an accurately sized square. This also helps you center the motif within the square.

The most common Wilendur design is the repeating three-across (*Dogwood* tablecloth, page 13, and *Rose Sprays* tablecloth, page 18). There can be nine to twelve motifs available, depending on the size of the tablecloth.

NOTE *Typically these designs contain mirror-imaged motifs on the sides and a different version of the motif in the vertical center row. When creating your quilt, you will want to pay attention to the orientation of the motifs.*

Other types of designs you might find are ones featuring:

 Four-corner bouquets (*Dena's Delight* tablecloth, page 15, and *Daisy Vase* tablecloth, page 16).

 Same size of blocks all over, containing two or more repeating designs (*Moda Fruit Basket* tablecloth, page 14).

 Only a border design. There are scenes with people that feature common European or Southwestern themes. You will see kitchen gadgets, pottery, and nature scenes with ducks and fish, such as those used to make *Field & Stream*, page 17.

 Large center motifs of fruit or flower bouquets or single designs filling the entire tablecloth (*Nostalgic Wholecloth* tablecloth, page 14).

 Unique designs (*Blue Roses* tablecloth, page 19, and *Vintage Roses* tablecloth, page 18).

Many tablecloths were produced in more than one colorway, which you could combine into one spectacular quilt.

When combining quilts, sometimes the white backgrounds may not match. One could be very white and the other more yellowed. Never bleach the tablecloths, but you could tea stain the one with the white background to better match the yellower one. They don't have to match exactly—they just have to blend.

Just use your imagination. With all the beautiful designs and colors to choose from, it is easy to find sections to showcase in a quilt. Look at the examples on the next pages for twelve possibilities to get your creative juices flowing.

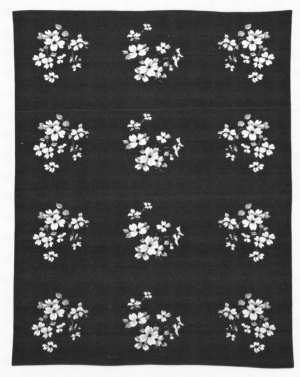

Original tablecloth

Dogwood quilt (page 28)

Original tablecloth

Baltimore Beauty quilt (page 33)

Original tablecloth

Nostalgic Wholecloth quilt (page 40)

Original tablecloth

Moda Fruit Basket quilt (page 44)

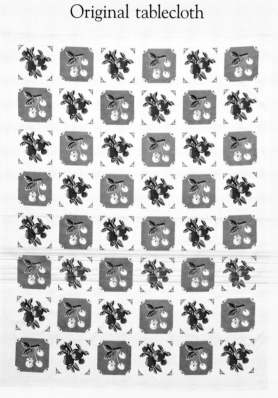

Original tablecloth #1

Original tablecloth #2

Dena's Delight quilt (page 49)

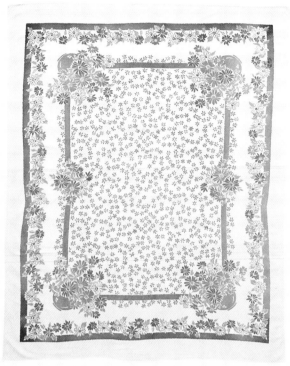

Original tablecloth

Daisy Vase quilt (page 54)

Original tablecloth

Mums quilt (page 64)

Original tablecloth #1

Original tablecloth #2

Field & Stream quilt (page 58)

Original tablecloth

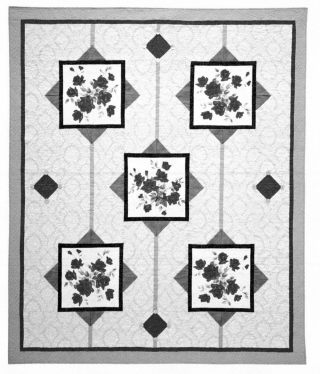

Rosesprays quilt (page 71)

Original tablecloth

Vintage Roses quilt (page 77)

Original tablecloth

Blue Roses quilt (page 82)

Original tablecloth

Original tablecloth

Delicate Daisies quilt (page 88)

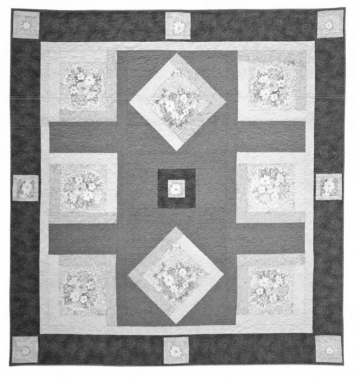

Color Palette
and Fabric Choices

How amazing are the fabric choices today? There's so much to choose from. So decide what feel you want your tablecloth quilt to have. You can go with vintage reproduction fabrics, batiks, or contemporary prints. Keep in mind that the focus of these quilts is the tablecloth art, so build around that.

Dogwood incorporates some reproduction vintage fabrics with a dramatic graphic design using black and white. A slightly tea-stained fabric creates the aged look I wanted for one of the fabrics. Notice the robin's-egg blue border around the dogwood motif. Although that color does not appear in the actual tablecloth, it picks up the soft pearl grays in the flowers. Look for those subtle colors to accent your palette.

Rosesprays has a very classic vintage look. The background resembles Victorian wallpaper with soft vertical stripes. This both showcases the vivid colors of the roses and subdues the overall look. Adding prairie points and vintage buttons makes this quilt look like a beautifully wrapped present!

Detail of *Rosesprays* (page 71)

Detail of *Dogwood* (page 28)

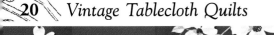

The lively reproduction prints used for *Moda Fruit Basket* resemble the bright reds and milky jade glass used in 1950s kitchens.

Detail of *Moda Fruit Basket* (page 44)

We used hot, bright contemporary-colored fabrics to accent the two tablecloths used in *Dena's Delight*.

Detail of *Dena's Delight* (page 49)

The intense blue and green batiks chosen for *Blue Roses* give this quilt an exotic look.

Detail of *Blue Roses* (page 82)

Color Palette and Fabric Choices **21**

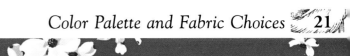

Because of the strong autumn colors in *Baltimore Beauty*, we decided to use a monochromatic palette of beige, white, and yellow. It softens these muddy colors from the '60s.

Detail of *Baltimore Beauty* (page 33)

Auditioning Fabrics

For me the process of choosing fabrics almost always starts with the computer. Being a fine artist and graphic designer, I like to see as many of the elements together as possible. I start by taking a digital photo of a section of the tablecloth. I place the image in an image-based software program (such as Photoshop) and crop it to the area I want to use.

Next, I choose a fabric manufacturer's website and begin to select the colors I feel will work with the tablecloth. This helps me decide what direction I will take with the quilt (Victorian, modern, sophisticated, playful). I place the swatches next to the tablecloth image and can then begin to visualize the design, feel, and color.

You can follow a similar process by auditioning fabrics from your stash with your tablecloth and then going to the quilt shop to fill in what is missing.

Embellishments

Back to your drawers, the flea market, or fabric stores to search for buttons, beads, and other trinkets to accessorize your quilt. Don't forget about handmade fabric flowers, prairie points, rickrack, and appliqué motifs. Just have fun.

Quilt Labels

Be sure to make a label to add to the back of your quilt to document the origins of the tablecloths, especially if there is any historical family information. Future generations will love to read about any background information you care to share about making the quilt. It gives them a close tie to the maker—you!

Detail of *Nostalgic Wholecloth* (page 40)

Detail of *Baltimore Beauty* (page 33)

Detail of *Daisy Vase* (page 54)

Details of *Rosesprays* (page 71)

Detail of *Vintage Roses* (page 77)

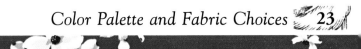

How to Use the Project Instructions

Now that you have some thoughts about tablecloth possibilities, you have a few options for creating your quilt.

Option 1: Choose to make
Moda Fruit Basket (page 44)

The tablecloth in this quilt is currently available to purchase online from Moda Home (www.homealamode .com/tablecloths.aspx) as are other tablecloths with different motifs in similar layouts. However, there is no guarantee how long that will be the case.

Option 2: Work with the project instructions as written

1. Count the motifs to see how many the tablecloth will yield. Measure the motifs, and write down the minimum and maximum sizes you can cut them.

2. The quilt projects are arranged in order of cut tablecloth-motif sizes. Look through the projects and determine which ones match the cut size of your motifs. Choose your favorite and follow the instructions. If you don't find any projects that match exactly, or prefer a different project that doesn't match your cut motif size, go to Option 3.

Option 3: Modify the motif size to fit your motifs

When you are following the project instructions, the only thing you will have to change is the cut size of the tablecloth motif and the block frames. Because the block size will be the same as in the instructions, all the other instructions will work as written.

1. Measure your tablecloth motifs and write down the minimum and maximum sizes you can cut them.

2. Look through the projects and determine which ones include a cut motif size that fits within your minimum/maximum size range from Step 1 and choose your favorite.

3. On graph paper, draw a square the finished block size given in the project instructions. Use 1 square on the graph paper to equal 1″ on the quilt block. Example: For a 16½″ × 16½″ unfinished block, subtract ½″ to draw a 16″ × 16″ block of 16 squares across and 16 squares down.

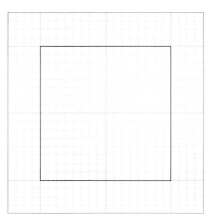

Draw square 16″ × 16″ on graph paper.

Most of the blocks in the projects have a small frame around the motif. All you have to do is adjust the size of the frame so that the block size in the project instructions works for your motif size. If the block in the project instructions doesn't include a frame, and your motif is smaller than the unfinished block size, you will create a frame to achieve the block size given in the project instructions. It's not hard, really.

4. Look at the minimum and maximum sizes you wrote down in Step 1. Example: The size you can cut your motifs is a minimum of 10″ × 10″ and a maximum of 13″ × 13″.

5. Look at the size of the drawn square, determine what size you want the finished motif (the finished size is the cut size minus ½″ for seam allowances), and draw this smaller square centered in the larger square. The space between the 2 squares will be the finished width of the block frames. Example: I want a 12″ × 12″ finished motif size. This will give me a 2″ finished block frame.

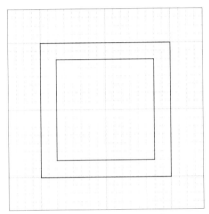

Draw finished motif size on graph paper.

6. To create your 16½″ × 16½″ unfinished block (finished block size plus ½″ for seam allowances) using a 12½″ × 12½″ cut motif (finished motif size plus ½″ for seam allowances), cut the block frame strips 2½″ × fabric width (finished frame width plus ½″ for seam allowances).

7. Trim 2 pieces 2½″ × the length of the sides of the motif (12½″ for this example).

8. Sew them to the sides of the cut motif. Press.

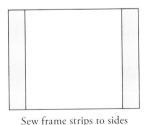

Sew frame strips to sides of motif. Press.

9. Measure the block from side to side and trim 2 pieces to 2½″ × this measurement (16½″ for this example).

10. Sew them to the top and bottom of the block. Press.

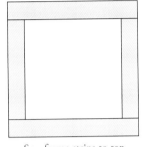

Sew frame strips to top and bottom. Press.

Alternatively, here is a mathematical way to determine the cut sizes of the block frame strips, with no drawing involved.

1. To determine the width of the fabric strips, calculate:

Block size (unfinished) – motif size (cut) ÷ 2 (for both sides) + ½″ (for seam allowances). Example: 16½″ × 18½″ block size (unfinished) and 12″ × 16″ motif size (cut)

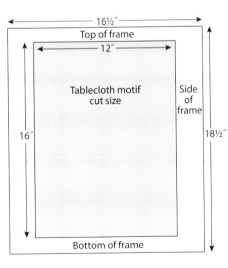

Top of frame — 16½″

12″

Tablecloth motif cut size

Side of frame

16″   18½″

Bottom of frame

Using width measurement:

16½″ – 12″ = 4½″

4½″ ÷ 2 = 2¼″

2¼″ + ½″ = 2¾″ cut strip width for the frame sides

Using height measurement:

18½″ – 16″ = 2½″

2½″ ÷ 2 = 1¼″

1¼″ + ½″ = 1¾″ strip width to cut for the top and bottom of the frame

2. Determining the length of each strip to cut is even simpler. For the side (vertical) frame strips, the cut length is equal to the height of the motif size (cut).

For the top and bottom (horizontal) frame strips, the cut length equals the width of the block size unfinished.

3. Sew the frame strips to the motif following Step 8 and Step 10 above.

NOTE *For all projects, we recommend labeling your cut fabrics with the letter designations in each cutting list to make assembly easier.*

Section Two:
Making the Quilts

Dogwood

Designed and pieced by Rose Sheifer, quilted by Darla Padilla

White print

Blue

Black print

Pale yellow

Red

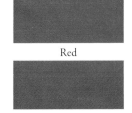

Finished size: 68½″ × 68½″ | **Block size (unfinished):** 16½″ × 16½″

Tablecloth motif size (cut): 12½″ × 12½″

The sashing and borders frame the tablecloth motifs to create this sophisticated design. Make it bold and graphic or soft and sophisticated—whatever matches the style of your tablecloth.

FABRIC REQUIREMENTS

Based on 42″ fabric width.

Tablecloth motifs: 9 squares 12½″ × 12½″ for blocks (A)

White print: 2 yards for block frames and lengthwise-cut outer border (1⅔ yards for crosswise-cut and pieced border)

Blue: ⅝ yard for block frames

Black print: 1 yard for sashing and outer border corners

Pale yellow: 2 yards for sashing and lengthwise-cut inner border (¾ yard for crosswise-cut and pieced border)

Red: ⅝ yard for binding

Backing: 73″ × 73″

Batting: 73″ × 73″

CUTTING

White print
Cut the border strips first on the lengthwise grain.

Cut 4 lengthwise strips 4½″ × 60½″ for the outer border (O and P).

From the remainder:
Cut 18 strips 2″ × 12½″ (B).

Cut 18 strips 2″ × 15½″ (C).

Blue
Cut 18 strips 1″ × fabric width; subcut into:
    18 strips 1″ × 15½″ (D) and
    18 strips 1″ × 16½″ (E).

Black print
Cut 5 strips 2½″ × fabric width; subcut into:
    16 strips 2½″ × 5½″ (F) and
    4 strips 2½″ × 12½″ (H).

Cut 5 strips 3½″ × fabric width; subcut into:
    4 strips 3½″ × 5½″ (I),
    8 strips 3½″ × 12½″ (K), and
    4 strips 3½″ × 8½″ (L).

Cut 4 squares 4½″ × 4½″ (Q).

Pale yellow
Cut the border strips first on the lengthwise grain.

Cut 2 lengthwise strips 1½″ × 58½″ for the inner border (M).

Cut 2 lengthwise strips 1½″ × 60½″ for the inner border (N).

From the remainder:
Cut 3 strips 2½″ × fabric width (approximately 36″); subcut into:
    12 strips 2½″ × 6½″ (G).

Cut 3 strips 3½″ × fabric width; subcut into:
    12 strips 3½″ × 6½″ (J).

Red
Cut 8 strips 2¼″ × fabric width for the binding.

Blocks

Use ¼″ seam allowances.

1. Sew B strips to each side of an A square. Press.

2. Sew C strips to the top and bottom edges of A. Press.

3. Sew D strips to each side of the block. Press.

4. Sew E strips to the top and bottom edges of the block. Press.

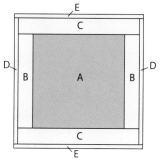

Sew frame strips to block.

5. Repeat Steps 1–4 to make 9 blocks.

Construction

1. Sew together F/G/F to construct a 2½″ vertical sashing unit. Press. Make 6.

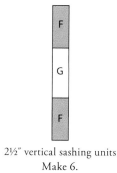

2½″ vertical sashing units
Make 6.

2. Sew the blocks into rows with the 2½″ vertical sashing units between the blocks. Press.

3. Sew together F/G/H/G/H/G/F to construct a 2½″ horizontal sashing strip. Press. Make 2.

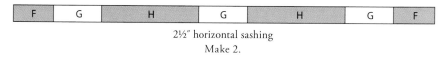

2½″ horizontal sashing
Make 2.

4. Sew the rows together with the 2½″ horizontal sashing strips between the rows. Press.

5. Sew together I/J/K/J/K/J/I to construct a 3½″ horizontal pieced border. Press. Make 2.

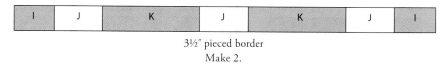

3½″ pieced border
Make 2.

6. Sew the 3½″ horizontal pieced borders to the top and bottom edges of the quilt top. Press.

Borders

1. Add an M strip to each side of the quilt top. Press.

2. Add N strips to the top and bottom edges of the quilt top. Press.

3. Add an O strip to each side of the quilt top. Press.

4. Sew a Q square to each end of a P strip. Press. Make 2.

5. Add Q/P/Q strips to the top and bottom edges of the quilt top. Press.

7. Sew together L/J/K/J/K/J/L to construct a 3½″ vertical pieced border. Press. Make 2.

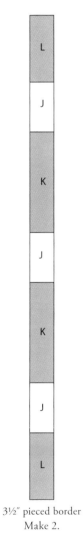

3½″ pieced border
Make 2.

8. Sew the 3½″ pieced borders to the sides of the quilt top. Press.

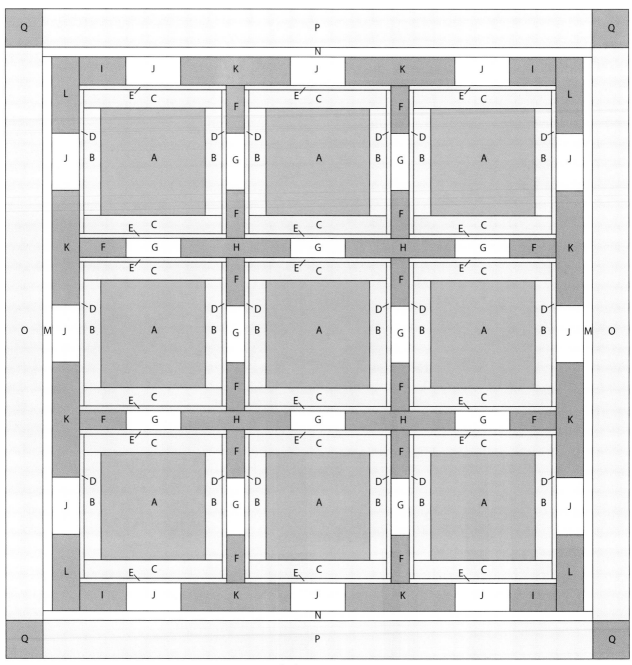

Quilt construction

Finishing
Layer, baste, quilt, bind, and label your quilt.

Baltimore Beauty

Designed and pieced by Rose Sheifer, quilted by Darla Padilla

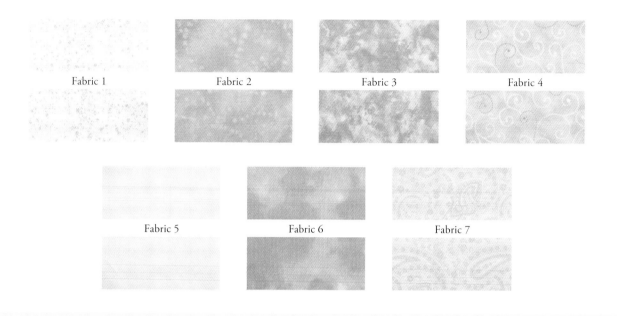

Fabric 1   Fabric 2   Fabric 3   Fabric 4

Fabric 5   Fabric 6   Fabric 7

Finished size: 67½″ × 91½″ | **Block size (unfinished):** 24½″ × 24½″, 36½″ × 36½″

Tablecloth motif sizes (cut): 12½″ × 12½″, 16½″ × 16½″

Fussy cut the small blocks from a printed fabric or the print of the tablecloth, or you can appliqué motifs onto a background square Broderie Perse style. Mix the different-sized motifs to make this creative design. Be sure to label the fabrics and cut pieces to keep them organized.

FABRIC REQUIREMENTS

Based on 42″ fabric width.

Tablecloth motifs: 4 squares 12½″ × 12½″ (A1) and 1 square 16″ × 16″ (A2) for blocks

Fabric 1: ⅜ yard for fabric flowers (optional)

Fabric 2: 1 yard for corner block frames and Block 1

Fabric 3: ½ yard for center block frame and Block 1

Fabric 4: 2½ yards for center block triangles, Blocks 1 and 2, outer border, and binding

Fabric 5: ½ yard for center block frame, Block 1, and Block 2

Fabric 6: 1 yard for center block frame, Block 2, and inner border

Fabric 7: ⅞ yard for corner block frames and Blocks 1 and 2

Print: ⅜ yard or 4 fussy-cut motifs for Block 2 (We were able to fussy cut the leaves from the tablecloth.)

Backing: 73″ × 97″

Batting: 73″ × 97″

1″ buttons (optional): 6 for flower centers

24-gauge wire (optional): 6 pieces 20″ long for flowers

CUTTING

Fabric 1

Cut 3 strips 3½″ × fabric width; subcut into:
 6 strips 3½″ × 18″ for the flowers.

Fabric 2

Cut 2 strips 4½″ × fabric width; subcut into:
 4 strips 4½″ × 16½″ (D).

Cut 4 strips 4½″ × fabric width; subcut into:
 4 strips 4½″ × 24½″ (E).

Cut 2 strips 2½″ × fabric width; subcut into:
 6 strips 2½″ × 10½″ (N).

Fabric 3

Cut 2 strips 2½″ × fabric width; subcut into:
 6 strips 2½″ × 10½″ (O).

Cut 4 strips 2½″ × fabric width; subcut into:
 2 strips 2½″ × 32½″ (K) and
 2 strips 2½″ × 36½″ (L).

Fabric 4

Cut 1 strip 17″ × fabric width; subcut into:
 2 squares 17″ × 17″, and then cut in half diagonally (H).

Cut 2 strips 8½″ × fabric width; subcut into:
 6 squares 8½″ × 8½″ (M).

Cut 1 strip 2½″ × fabric width; subcut into:
 4 strips 2½″ × 10½″ (T).

Cut 5 strips 3″ × fabric width; piece into a long strip, and subcut into:
 2 strips 3″ × 86½″ for the side outer borders (Y).

Cut 4 strips 3″ × fabric width; piece into a continuous strip, and subcut into:
 2 strips 3″ × 67½″ for the top and bottom outer borders (Z).

Cut 9 strips 2¼″ × fabric width for the binding.

Fabric 5

Cut 2 strips 2″ × fabric width; subcut into:
 2 strips 2″ × 16½″ (F) and
 2 strips 2″ × 19½″ (G).

Cut 2 strips 2½″ × fabric width; subcut into:
 6 strips 2½″ × 10½″ (P).

Cut 1 strip 2½″ × fabric width; subcut into:
 4 strips 2½″ × 10½″ (V).

Fabric 6

Cut 4 strips 2½″ × fabric width; subcut into:
 2 strips 2½″ × 28½″ (I) and
 2 strips 2½″ × 32½″ (J).

Cut 1 strip 2½″ × fabric width; subcut into:
 4 strips 2½″ × 10½″ (U).

Cut 5 strips 1½″ × fabric width; piece into a long strip, and subcut into:
 2 strips 1½″ × 84½″ for the side inner borders (W).

Cut 3 strips 1½″ × fabric width; piece into a long strip, and subcut into:
 2 strips 1½″ × 62½″ for the top and bottom inner borders (X).

Fabric 7

Cut 7 strips 2½″ × fabric width; subcut into:
 8 strips 2½″ × 12½″ (B) and
 8 strips 2½″ × 16½″ (C).

Cut 2 strips 2½″ × fabric width; subcut into:
 6 strips 2½″ × 10½″ (Q).

Cut 1 strip 2½″ × fabric width; subcut into:
 4 strips 2½″ × 10½″ (S).

Print

Cut 1 strip 8½″ × fabric width; subcut into:
 4 squares 8½″ × 8½″ (R).

Blocks

Use ¼" seam allowances.

Corner Blocks

1. Sew B strips to the sides of an A1 square. Press.

2. Sew C strips to the top and bottom edges of A1. Press.

3. Sew D strips to the sides of the block. Press.

4. Sew E strips to the top and bottom edges of the block. Press.

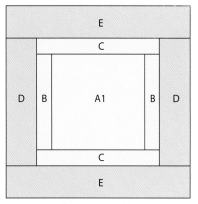

Sew strips to A1.

5. Repeat to make 4 blocks.

Center Block

1. Sew F strips to 2 sides of the A2 square. Press.

2. Sew G strips to the other 2 sides of A2. Press.

3. Sew an H triangle to one side of the block. Press.

4. Sew an H triangle to the opposite side of the block. Press.

5. Repeat Steps 3 and 4 to add the other H triangles to the block. Press.

6. Trim to 28½" × 28½", making sure the block is centered and symmetrical.

7. Add I strips to 2 sides of the block. Press.

8. Sew J strips to the other 2 sides of the block. Press.

9. Repeat Steps 7 and 8 to add the K and L strips to the block. Press.

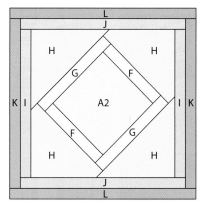

Center block piecing

Blocks 1 and 2

Please note that our blocks were made using a variety of fabrics, randomly pieced for a scrappy style. The instructions and quilt construction diagram below use a more repetitive style to simplify things. Sew strips N, O, P, and Q to the M squares using partial-seam piecing, varying the placement of the strips to suit your preference.

1. Sew the first strip to an M square with a partial seam. Press.

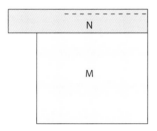

2. Add the second strip. Press.

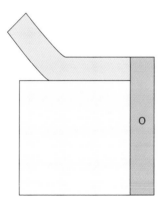

3. Add the third strip. Press.

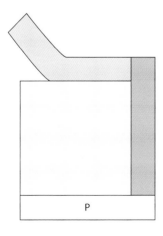

4. Add the fourth strip and finish the seam on the first strip. Press.

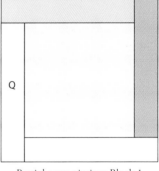

Partial-seam piecing; Block 1

5. Repeat Steps 1–4 to make a total of 6 Block 1s.

6. Repeat Steps 1–4 to sew strips S, T, U, and V to the R squares using partial-seam piecing, varying the placement of the strips to suit your preference. Press. Make 4 Block 2s.

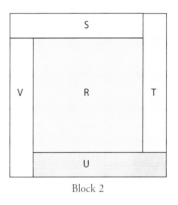

Block 2

Construction

1. Lay out the blocks according to the construction diagram (page 38).

2. Sew Blocks 1 and 2 together in columns. Press.

3. Sew the blocks together in horizontal sections. Press.

4. Sew the rows together. Press.

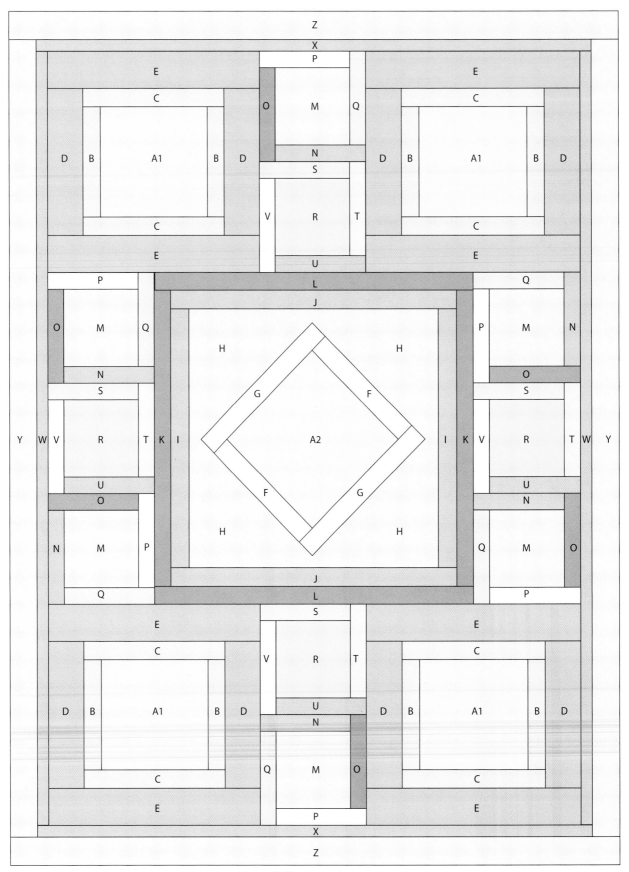

Quilt construction

Borders

1. Add a W strip to each side of the quilt top. Press.

2. Add X strips to the top and bottom of the quilt top. Press.

3. Add a Y strip to each side of the quilt top. Press.

4. Add Z strips to the top and bottom of the quilt top. Press.

Finishing

Layer, baste, quilt, bind, and label your quilt.

Fabric Flowers

1. Fold each of the short sides of a 3½" × 18" strip under ¼", press, and stitch ⅛" from the folds. Repeat for the long sides.

2. Insert a piece of wire into one of the channels of the long ends and curl the wire end to prevent it from slipping back in.

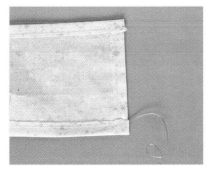

Fold sides under ¼".
Insert wire into channel.

3. Stitch a line of hand basting along the long side opposite the side with the wire.

Hand baste the opposite long side.

4. Pull one end of the basting stitches to gather the piece into a circle.

Gather into circle.

5. Hand stitch the 2 short sides, right sides together.

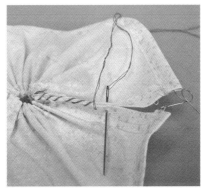

Stitch 2 short sides together.

6. Adjust the gathers to form an even circle.

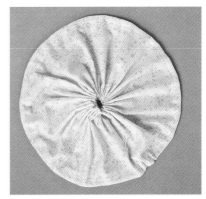

Adjust gathers.

7. Fold the wire edge of the flower under ¼" to the wrong side.

Fold wire edge to wrong side.

8. Repeat Steps 1–7 to make a total of 6 flowers.

9. Hand stitch the flowers to the quilt with a button at the center of each flower.

Attach with center button.

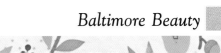

Nostalgic Wholecloth

Designed and pieced by Rose Sheifer, quilted by Jocelyn Marzan, and embellished by Liz Aneloski

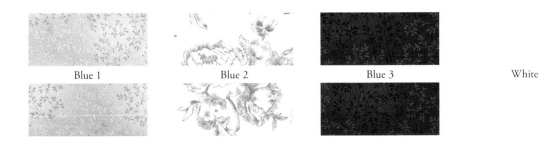

Blue 1   Blue 2   Blue 3   White

Finished size: 52½″ × 58½″ | **Tablecloth motif size (cut):** see guidance below

Because your tablecloth probably won't be the same size as ours, the instructions will guide you to modify the construction of the quilt based on the size of your tablecloth. The measurements for making the quilt with our tablecloth measurements are in parentheses. The fabric requirements for the borders and binding are based on a maximum cut tablecloth size of 42½″ × 48½″. If yours is larger, purchase extra fabric to make longer borders and binding.

Use the print of the tablecloth as inspiration for the quilting design in the center of the quilt and in the outer borders. We added tiny white buttons to give the quilt more texture and interest.

FABRIC REQUIREMENTS
Based on 42″ fabric width.

Tablecloth: Trim to an even number of inches plus ½″ for seam allowances in both directions. We used a 38½″ × 44½″ tablecloth.

Blue 1: ¼ yard for inner border

Blue 2: ¼ yard for inner border

Blue 3: ⅝ yard for inner border and binding

White: 1⅝ yards for lengthwise-cut outer border or 1 yard for crosswise-cut outer border

Backing: size of quilt top plus 4″ (57″ × 63″)

Batting: size of quilt top plus 4″ (57″ × 63″)

CUTTING

Blue 1
Cut 2 strips 2½″ × fabric width for the inner border.

Blue 2
Cut 2 strips 2½″ × fabric width for the inner border.

Blue 3
Cut 2 strips 2½″ × fabric width for the inner border.

Cut enough strips 2¼″ × fabric width to go around your quilt (6) plus at least 18″ extra for the binding.

White
After you have sewn on the pieced borders, measure the length of your quilt top vertically through the center of the quilt top, and cut 2 lengthwise strips 5½″ × this measurement (48½″) for the side outer borders.

Then measure the quilt top horizontally across the center, add 10″ to accommodate the side outer borders, and cut 2 lengthwise strips 5½″ × this measurement (52½″) for the top and bottom outer borders.

Border Construction

Use ¼" seam allowances.

Inner Borders

1. Sew the 6 blue strips together, alternating the fabrics.

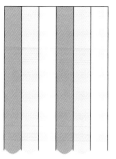

Sew strips together.

2. Cut the strip set into 2½" units.

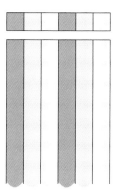

Cut strip set into units.

3. Measure the sides of the quilt top; the quilt length should be an even number; add ½" for seam allowances.

4. Sew the units together to equal the length needed for the sides. You might have to remove one or more squares.

5. Add the side inner borders to the quilt top. Press.

6. Measure the top edges and the bottom edges of the quilt top; the quilt width should be an even number; add ½" for seam allowances.

7. Sew the units together to equal the length needed for the top and bottom edges. You might have to remove one or more squares.

8. Add the top and bottom inner borders. Press.

Outer Borders

1. Measure and cut the border strips, referring to the instructions in Cutting (page 41).

2. Add the side outer border strips to the sides of the quilt top. Press.

3. Add the top and bottom outer border strips to the top and bottom of the quilt top. Press.

Quilt construction

Finishing
Layer, baste, quilt, bind, and label your quilt.

Moda Fruit Basket

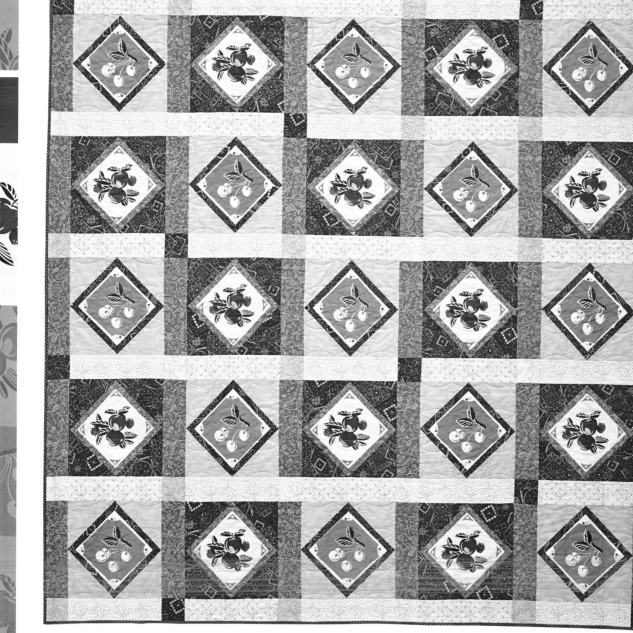

Designed and pieced by Rose Sheifer, quilted by Darla Padilla

Red bandana print

Blue texture print

Blue with white dots

White with blue dots

White with red dots

Cream

Red with white dots

Finished size: 78½″ × 78½″ | **Block size (unfinished):** 12½″ × 12½″

Tablecloth motif size (cut): 7½″ × 7½″

Recombine the two different blocks from this Moda Home reproduction tablecloth and add sashing for a wonderful, simple quilt.

FABRIC REQUIREMENTS

Based on 42″ fabric width.

Tablecloth motifs: 13 squares 7½″ × 7½″ for Block A's and 12 squares 7½″ × 7½″ for Block B's

Red bandana print: 1¾ yards for Block A frames, Block B background, and cornerstones

Blue texture print: 1½ yards for Block B frames and vertical sashing

Blue with white dots: 1¾ yards for Block A background and cornerstones

White with blue dots: ⅝ yard for horizontal sashing

White with red dots: ⅝ yard for horizontal sashing

Cream: ¼ yard for cornerstones

Red with white dots: ⅝ yard for binding

Backing: 83″ × 83″

Batting: 83″ × 83″

CUTTING

Red bandana print

Cut 13 strips 1¼″ × fabric width; subcut into:
   26 strips 1¼″ × 7½″ (C) and
   26 strips 1¼″ × 9″ (D).

Cut 5 strips 8″ × fabric width; subcut into:
   24 squares 8″ × 8″, and then cut each in
   half diagonally (H).

Cut 1 strip 3½″ × fabric width; subcut into:
   10 squares 3½″ × 3½″ (K).

Blue texture print

Cut 11 strips 1¼″ × fabric width; subcut into:
   24 strips 1¼″ × 7½″ (E) and
   24 strips 1¼″ × 9″ (F).

Cut 10 strips 3½″ × fabric width; subcut into:
   30 strips 3½″ × 12½″ (I).

Blue with white dots

Cut 6 strips 8″ × fabric width; subcut into:
   26 squares 8″ × 8″, and then cut each in
   half diagonally (G).

Cut 2 strips 3½″ × fabric width; subcut into:
   15 squares 3½″ × 3½″ (K).

White with blue dots

Cut 5 strips 3½″ × fabric width; subcut into:
   15 strips 3½″ × 12½″ (J).

White with red dots

Cut 5 strips 3½″ × fabric width; subcut into:
   15 strips 3½″ × 12½″ (J).

Cream texture print

Cut 1 strip 3½″ × fabric width; subcut into:
   11 squares 3½″ × 3½″ (K).

Red with white dots

Cut 9 strips 2¼″ × fabric width for the binding.

Blocks

Use ¼″ seam allowances.

1. Sew a C strip to each side of an A square. Press.

2. Sew D strips to the top and bottom edges of A. Press.

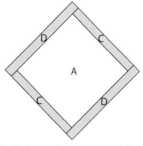

Block A; sew frame strips to block.

3. Sew a G triangle, centered, to one side of the block. (Triangles are cut oversized and trimmed later.) Press.

4. Sew a G triangle to the opposite side of the block. Press.

5. Repeat Steps 3 and 4 to add G triangles to the other sides of the block. Press.

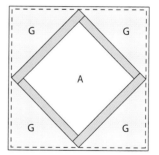

Block A; sew triangles to block and trim; make 13.

6. Trim to 12½″ × 12½″, making sure the block is centered and symmetrical. Make 13 blocks.

7. Sew an E strip to each side of a B square. Press.

8. Sew F strips to the top and bottom edges of B. Press.

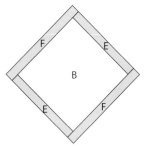

Block B; sew frame strips to block.

9. Sew an H triangle to one side of the block. Press.

10. Sew an H triangle to the opposite side of the block. Press.

11. Repeat Steps 9 and 10 to add H triangles to the other sides of the block. Press.

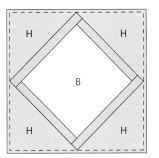

Block B; sew triangles to block and trim; make 12.

12. Trim to 12½″ × 12½″, making sure the block is centered and symmetrical. Make 12 blocks.

Construction

1. Lay out the blocks, sashing strips, and cornerstones following the quilt construction diagram or as you please.

2. Sew the blocks into horizontal rows with I strips between them.

3. Sew the J strips and K squares into horizontal rows.

4. Sew the rows together.

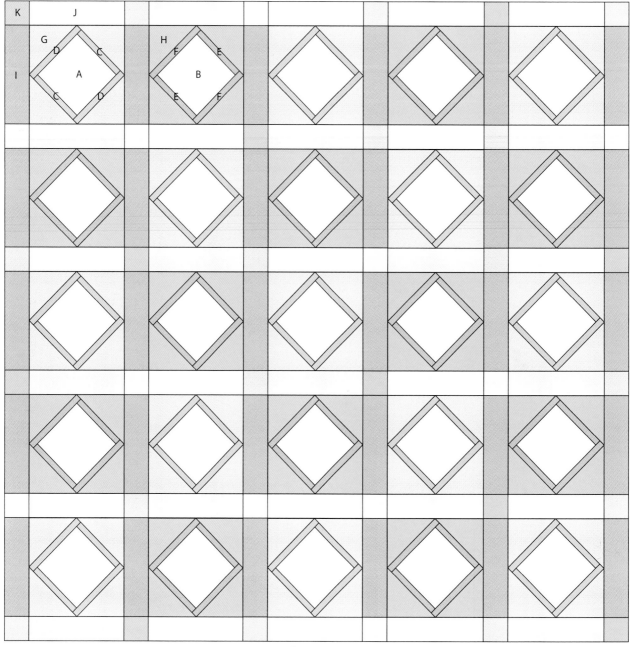

Quilt construction

Finishing
Layer, baste, quilt, bind, and label your quilt.

Dena's Delight

Designed and pieced by Rose Sheifer, quilted by Darla Padilla

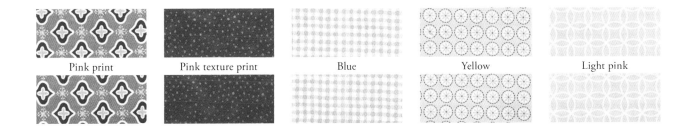

Pink print   Pink texture print   Blue   Yellow   Light pink

Finished size: 73½″ × 73½″ | **Block size (unfinished):** 13½″ × 13½″

Tablecloth motif size (cut): 13½″ × 13½″

Try combining elements of two or more tablecloths when the usable fabric is limited. The beautiful flower sprays of these two tablecloths work well with each other. You will find similar colors and art imagery in many tablecloths. We pulled this quilt together by incorporating bright contemporary fabrics and geometric designs.

FABRIC REQUIREMENTS

Based on 42″ fabric width.

Tablecloth motifs: 8 squares
13½″ × 13½″ (A) for blocks

Pink print: 1⅝ yards for center block, large corner triangles, and border squares

Pink texture print: ⅝ yard for center block and sashing

Blue: 1½ yards for center block, inner border, outer border, and binding

Yellow: 2 yards for center block, large corner triangles, and border squares

Light pink: 1 yard for large corner triangles

Lightweight fusible interfacing
(Make It Simpler fusible interfacing strips by C&T Publishing): 6 strips 1½″ × 45″

Backing: 78″ × 78″

Batting: 78″ × 78″

CUTTING

Pink print

Cut the pieces in the following order:

Cut 1 square 32″ × 32″, and then cut as directed in Construction (page 53) (F).

Cut 5 strips 4″ × fabric width for the border squares.

Cut 1 square 5″ × 5″ (B).

Pink texture print

Cut 1 strip 5″ × fabric width; subcut into:
    2 squares 5″ × 5″, and then cut in half
    diagonally (C), and
    4 squares 4″ × 4″ (K).

Cut 2 strips 1½″ × fabric width; subcut into:
    6 strips 1½″ × 13½″ for the short sashing.

Cut 2 strips 1½″ × 41½″ for the long sashing.

Cut 2 strips 1½″ × 41½″ for the side sashing.

Cut 2 strips 1½″ × 43½″ for the top and bottom sashing, adding leftover pieces as necessary to achieve the required length.

Blue

Cut 1 strip 6½″ × fabric width; subcut into:
   2 squares 6½″ × 6½″, and then cut in half
   diagonally (D).

Cut 6 strips 2″ × fabric width; sew into
1 continuous strip and then subcut into:
   2 strips 2″ × 60½″ (I) and
   2 strips 2″ × 63½″ (J).

Cut 7 strips 2″ × fabric width; sew into
1 continuous strip, and then subcut into:
   2 strips 2″ × 70½″ (L) and
   2 strips 2″ × 73½″ (M).

Cut 8 strips 2¼″ × fabric width for the binding.

Yellow

Cut 1 square 32″ × 32″, and then cut
as directed in Construction (page 53);
you will use only 2 triangles (H).

Cut 1 strip 9″ × fabric width; subcut into:
   2 squares 9″ × 9″, and then cut each in half
   diagonally (E).

Cut 5 strips 4″ × fabric width for the border squares.

Light pink

Cut 1 square 32″ × 32″, and then cut as
directed below in Construction (page 53);
you will use only 2 triangles (G).

Center Block

Use ¼" seam allowances.

1. Sew a C triangle, centered, to one side of the B square. (Triangles are cut oversized and trimmed later.) Press.

2. Sew a C triangle to the opposite side of B. Press.

3. Repeat Steps 1 and 2 to add the remaining C triangles to the other sides of B.

4. Trim to 7″ × 7″, making sure the block is centered and symmetrical.

5. Repeat Steps 1–3 to add D triangles to the block. Press.

6. Trim to 9⅝″ × 9⅝″, making sure the block is centered and symmetrical.

7. Repeat Steps 1–3 to add E triangles to the block.

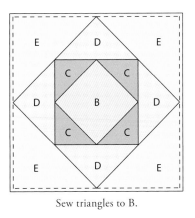

Sew triangles to B.

8. Trim to 13½″ × 13½″, making sure the block is centered and symmetrical.

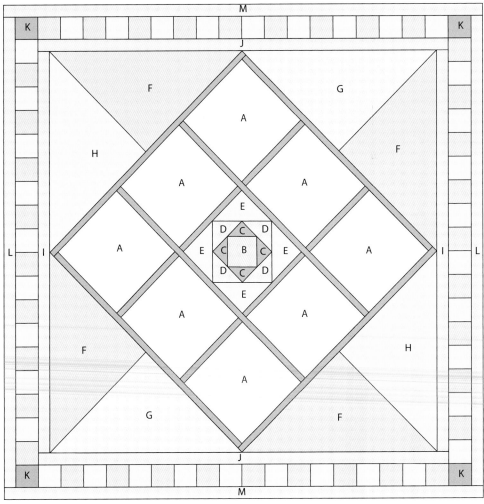

Quilt construction

Construction

1. Lay out the center block, table-cloth motifs, and sashing according to the quilt construction diagram (page 52).

2. Sew the center block and table-cloth motifs together in columns with short sashing strips between the blocks. Press.

3. Sew the columns together with the 41½″ long sashing strips between them. Press.

4. Add the 41½″ side sashing strips. Press.

5. Sew on the 43½″ top and bottom sashing strips. Press.

6. Fuse the interfacing strips diagonally from corner to corner, in both directions, across the wrong sides of the F, G, and H squares to stabilize the bias edges.

7. Cut the F, G, and H squares in half diagonally in both directions.

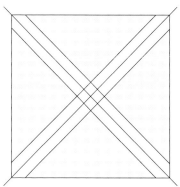

Fuse interfacing to wrong sides and cut diagonally in both directions.

8. Sew the F and G triangles together as shown, so they will be in the correct position. Press. Make 2.

9. Sew the F and H triangles together as shown, so they will be in the correct position. Press. Make 2.

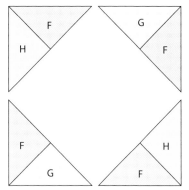

Sew F/G and F/H; make 2 of each.

10. Add an F/G unit to one side of the quilt top. Press.

11. Sew the other F/G unit to the opposite side of the quilt top. Press.

12. Repeat Steps 10 and 11 to add the F/H units to the other sides of the quilt top. Press.

13. Trim to 60½″ × 60½″, making sure the quilt top is centered and symmetrical. You should be trimming to ¼″ from the tips of the corners of the sashing.

Borders

Inner Borders

1. Sew the side inner borders to the quilt top. Press.

2. Add the top and bottom inner borders. Press.

Outer Borders

1. Sew the 10 border strips together, alternating the fabrics. Press.

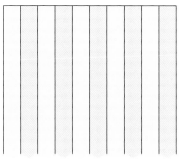

Sew border strips together.

2. Cut into 8 strip sets 4″ wide.

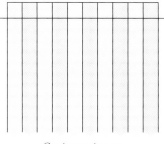

Cut into strip sets.

3. Sew the strip sets together in pairs to make 4 borders.

4. Remove 2 squares from each of the borders. Sew 2 borders to the sides of the quilt top. Press.

5. Sew a K square to each end of the 2 remaining borders. Press.

6. Sew the remaining 2 borders to the top and bottom of the quilt top. Press.

7. Sew an L strip to each side of the quilt top. Press.

8. Sew M strips to the top and bottom of the quilt top. Press.

Finishing

Layer, baste, quilt, bind, and label your quilt.

Daisy Vase

Designed and pieced by Rose Sheifer, quilted by Darla Padilla

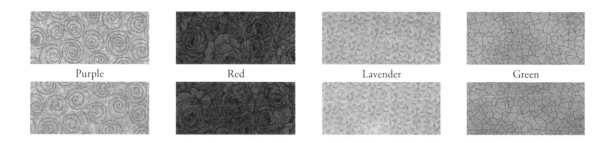

Purple | Red | Lavender | Green

Finished size: 41½″ × 41½″ | **Block size (unfinished):** 12½″ × 12½″

Tablecloth motif size (cut): 12½″ × 12½″

This is a great project to make if you have only one usable motif or just one cloth napkin.
Use a printed fabric or a background print from your tablecloth for the small blocks.

FABRIC REQUIREMENTS

Based on 42″ fabric width.

Tablecloth motifs: 1 square 12½″ × 12½″ (A) for center block

Print: ¼ yard for small squares (We were able to use the small print from the tablecloth.)

Purple: ⅝ yard for block frames and setting triangles

Red: ⅞ yard for blocks and outer border

Lavender: ½ yard for large block frames and inner border

Green: ⅜ yard for binding

Backing: 46″ × 46″

Batting: 46″ × 46″

Rickrack (optional): approximately 5½ yards of ¼″-wide and 4¼ yards of ½″-wide

CUTTING

Print
Cut 4 squares 5½″ × 5½″ (B).

Purple
Cut 2 squares 9⅜″ × 9⅜″, and then cut in half diagonally (I).

Cut 1 square 18¼″ × 18¼″, and then cut in quarters diagonally (J).

Red
Cut 2 strips 3″ × 36½″ for the side outer borders (M).

Cut 2 strips 3″ × 41½″ for the top and bottom outer borders (N).

Cut 5 strips 3″ × fabric width; subcut into:
    8 strips 3″ × 6½″ (E) and
    8 strips 3″ × 11½″ (F).

Lavender
Cut 3 strips 1″ × fabric width; subcut into:
    8 strips 1″ × 5½″ (C) and
    8 strips 1″ × 6½″ (D).

Cut 6 strips 1″ × fabric width; subcut into:
    8 strips 1″ × 11½″ (G) and
    8 strips 1″ × 12½″ (H).

Cut 4 strips 1½″ × fabric width; subcut into:
    2 strips 1½″ × 34½″ (K) and
    2 strips 1½″ × 36½″ (L).

Green
Cut 5 strips 2¼″ × fabric width for the binding.

Blocks

Use ¼″ seam allowances.

1. Sew a C strip to each side of a B square. Press.

2. Sew D strips to the top and bottom edges of B. Press.

3. Sew an E strip to each side of the block. Press.

4. Sew F strips to the top and bottom edges of the block. Press.

5. Sew a G strip to each side of the block. Press.

6. Sew H strips to the top and bottom edges of the block. Press.

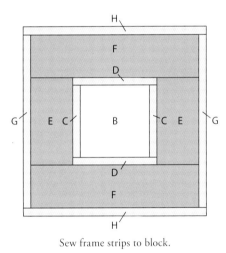

Sew frame strips to block.

7. Repeat Steps 1–6 to make 4 blocks.

Construction

1. Lay out the blocks and setting triangles according to the quilt construction diagram (page 57).

2. Sew the blocks and setting triangles together in diagonal rows. Press.

3. Sew the diagonal rows together. Press.

Borders

Inner Borders

1. Add a K strip to each side of the quilt top. Press.

2. Add L strips to the top and bottom edges of the quilt top. Press.

Outer Borders

1. Add an M strip to each side of the quilt top. Press.

2. Add N strips to the top and bottom edges of the quilt top. Press.

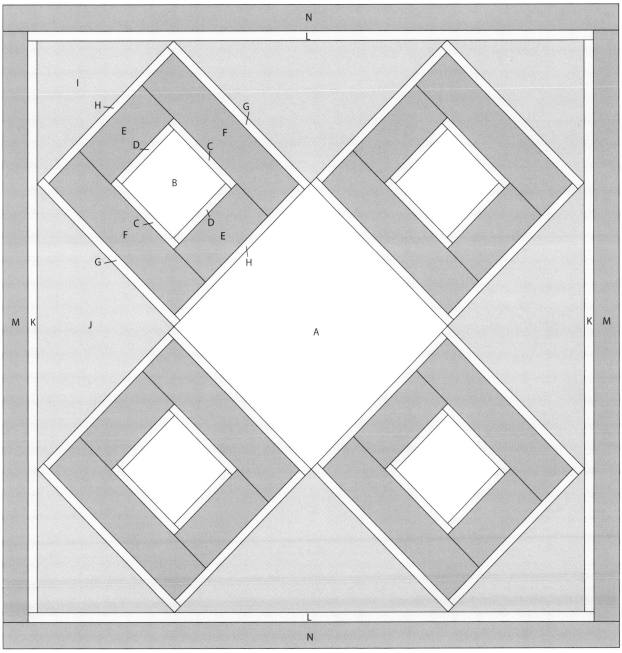

Quilt construction

Finishing

Layer, baste, quilt, bind, and label your quilt. Embellish with rickrack.

Field & Stream

Designed and pieced by Rose Sheifer, quilted by Darla Padilla

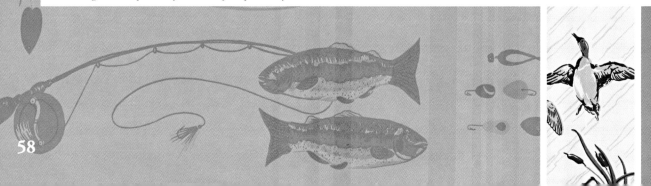

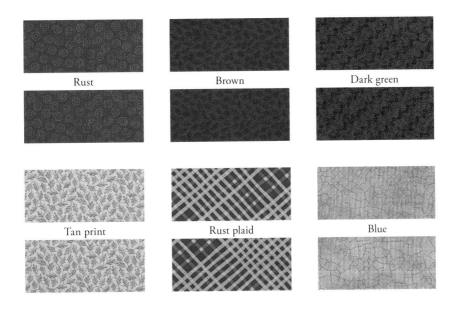

Rust

Brown

Dark green

Tan print

Rust plaid

Blue

Finished size: *75½″ × 65½″* | **Block size (unfinished):** *14½″ × 12″, 14½″ × 9½″, 14½″ × 14″*
Tablecloth motif sizes (cut): *10″ × 10″, 10″ × 7½″, 8″ × 12″, 12½″ × 12½″, 5½″ × 4½″, 5½″ × 7½″*

This quilt combines motifs from two different reproduction tablecloths from Moda Home. The surrounding Flying Geese blocks in the border tie the design together. Create the appliqué pattern to match your tablecloth by tracing an element from its design.

FABRIC REQUIREMENTS

Based on 42″ fabric width.

Tablecloth motifs: 11 pieces in varying sizes for blocks:

2 squares 10″ × 10″ (A1)

2 rectangles 10″ × 7½″ (A2)

2 rectangles 8″ × 12″ (A3)

2 squares 12½″ × 12½″ (A4)

2 rectangles 5½″ × 4½″ (A5)

1 rectangle 5½″ × 7½″ (A6)

Rust: 1⅛ yards for center section block background and sashing

Brown: 1⅛ yards for block frames, geese, and binding

Dark green: 1 yard for block frames and geese

Tan print: 1¾ yards for side section sashing, geese, and border corners

Rust plaid: 1 yard for vertical sashing, appliqués (optional), and geese

Blue: 1½ yards for Flying Geese background and border corners

CUTTING

Rust

Cut 1 strip 4″ × fabric width; subcut into:

4 rectangles 4″ × 4½″ (J).

Cut 1 strip 3″ × fabric width; subcut into:

2 rectangles 3″ × 5½″ (K).

Cut 1 strip 3½″ × fabric width; subcut into:

2 strips 3½″ × 12½″ (L).

Cut 2 strips 3″ × fabric width; subcut into:

4 strips 3″ × 12½″ (M).

Cut 3 strips 3″ × fabric width; piece into 1 long strip, and subcut into:

2 strips 3″ × 53½″ (O).

Cut 6 strips 1½″ × fabric width; piece into 1 long strip, and subcut into:

2 strips 1½″ × 53½″ for the side inner borders (Q) and
2 strips 1½″ × 65½″ for the top and bottom inner borders (R).

Brown

Cut 1 strip 2¾″ × fabric width; subcut into:

4 strips 2¾″ × 7½″ (D).

Cut 2 strips 1½″ × fabric width; subcut into:

4 strips 1½″ × 14½″ (E).

Cut 4 strips 3″ × fabric width; subcut into:

24 rectangles 3″ × 5½″ for the geese.

Cut 8 strips 2¼″ × fabric width for the binding.

Dark green

Cut 1 strip 2¾″ × fabric width; subcut into:

4 strips 2¾″ × 10″ (B).

Cut 2 strips 1½″ × fabric width; subcut into:

4 strips 1½″ × 14½″ (C).

Cut 2 strips 3¾″ × fabric width; subcut into:

4 strips 3¾″ × 12″ (F).

Cut 2 strips 1½″ × fabric width; subcut into:

4 strips 1½″ × 14½″ (G).

Cut 4 strips 3″ × fabric width; subcut into:

26 rectangles 3″ × 5½″ for the geese.

Tan print

Cut 2 strips 3″ × fabric width; subcut into:

4 strips 3″ × 14½″ (H).

Cut 2 strips 7½″ × fabric width; subcut into:

4 strips 7½″ × 14½″ (I).

Cut 6 strips 3″ × fabric width; piece into 2 equal long strips, and subcut into:

4 strips 3″ × 53½″ (N).

Cut 4 strips 3″ × fabric width; subcut into:

24 rectangles 3″ × 5½″ for the geese.

Cut 2 strips 3″ × fabric width; subcut into:

16 squares 3″ × 3″ for the border corners.

Rust plaid

See template pattern on page 62.

Cut 3 strips 4½″ × fabric width; piece into 1 long strip, and subcut into:

2 strips 4½″ × 53½″ (P).

Cut 4 appliqués.

Cut 4 strips 3″ × fabric width; subcut into:

22 rectangles 3″ × 5½″ for the geese.

Blue

Cut 14 strips 3″ × fabric width; subcut into:

192 squares 3″ × 3″ for the Flying Geese backgrounds.

Cut 1 strip 5½″ × fabric width; subcut into:

4 squares 5½″ × 5½″ for the border corners.

Side Sections

Use ¼″ seam allowances.

1. Sew a B strip to each side of an A1 square. Press.

2. Sew C strips to the top and bottom of A1. Press. Make 2.

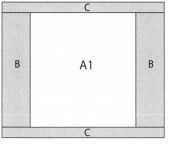

Block A1; make 2.

3. Sew a D strip to each side of an A2 rectangle. Press.

4. Sew E strips to the top and bottom of A2. Press. Make 2.

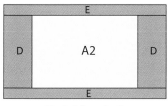

Block A2; make 2.

5. Sew an F strip to each side of an A3 rectangle. Press.

6. Sew G strips to the top and bottom of A3. Press. Make 2.

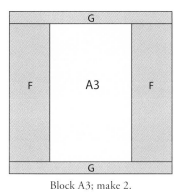

Block A3; make 2.

7. Lay out the A1, A2, and A3 blocks with the H and I sashing strips, following the quilt construction diagram.

8. Sew together to create a column. Press.

9. Sew an N strip to each side to complete a side section. Press. Make 2.

10. Position the appliqués, pin, and machine stitch ¹⁄₁₆″ from the raw edges, or appliqué by your preferred method.

Center Section

1. Sew a J rectangle to each side of an A5 rectangle. Press. Make 2.

2. Sew a K rectangle to each side of the A6 rectangle. Press.

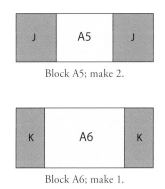

Block A5; make 2.

Block A6; make 1.

3. Lay out the A4, A5, and A6 blocks with the L and M sashing strips, following the quilt construction diagram.

4. Sew together to create a column.

5. Sew an O strip to each side to complete the center section. Press.

Construction

1. Sew the side and center sections together with the P sashing strips. Press.

2. Add a Q strip to each side of the quilt top. Press.

3. Add R strips to the top and bottom edges of the quilt top. Press.

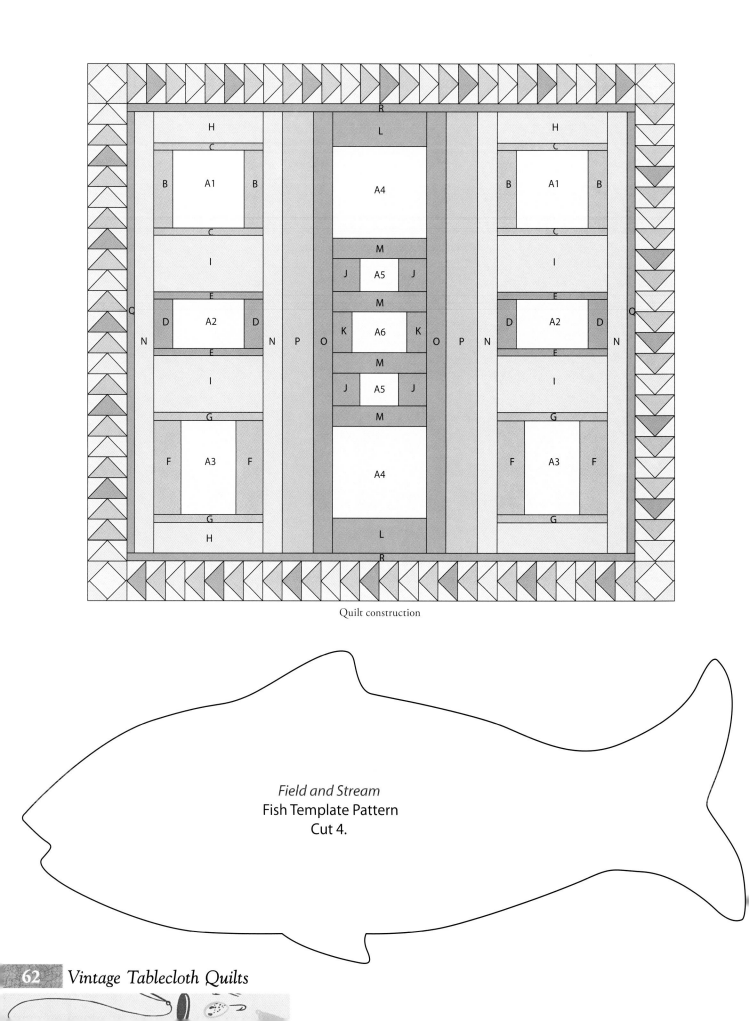

Quilt construction

Field and Stream
Fish Template Pattern
Cut 4.

Flying Geese Borders

1. Draw a line diagonally, from corner to corner, on the wrong side of each blue square.

2. Align a blue square with a short side of a geese rectangle, right sides together.

3. Sew on the marked line and trim, leaving a ¼″ seam allowance. Press.

Align square on rectangle. Sew on line and trim.

4. Repeat Steps 2 and 3 to sew a blue square to the other short side of the geese rectangle. Make 96. Trim to 3″ × 5½″, making sure the diagonal seams go to the corners and that there is a ¼″ seam allowance across the top of the block.

Add blue square to other short side. Make 96. Trim.

5. Draw a line diagonally, from corner to corner, on the wrong side of each tan border corner square.

6. Align a tan square with a corner of a blue border corner square, right sides together.

Align square on square. Sew on line and trim.

7. Sew on the marked line and trim, leaving a ¼″ seam allowance. Press.

8. Repeat Steps 6 and 7 to sew tan squares to the other 3 corners of the blue border corner square. Make 4. Trim to 5½″ × 5½″, making sure the seam allowances are even on each side of the block.

Add tan pieces to other corners. Make 4.

9. Referring to the photo for color placement, sew together 22 Flying Geese blocks for the side border. Press. The border should measure 55½″ long. Make 2.

10. Add these borders to the sides of the quilt top.

11. Sew together 26 Flying Geese blocks for the top border. Add a border corner square to each end. Press. The border should measure 65½″ long. Make 2.

12. Add these borders to the top and bottom of the quilt top.

Finishing

Layer, baste, quilt, bind, and label your quilt.

Mums

Designed and pieced by Rose Sheifer, quilted by Darla Padilla

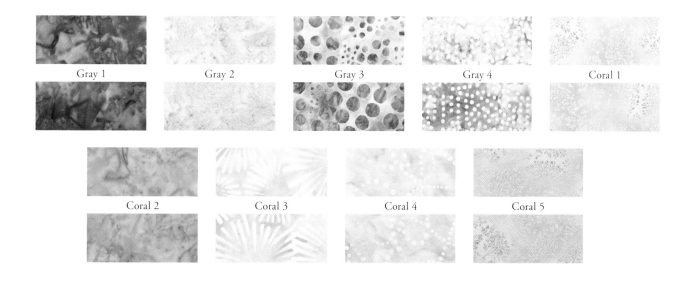

Gray 1 Gray 2 Gray 3 Gray 4 Coral 1

Coral 2 Coral 3 Coral 4 Coral 5

Finished size: 66½″ × 77½″ | **Block size (unfinished):** 16½″ × 18½″, 16½″ × 15½″

Tablecloth motif sizes (cut): 12″ × 14″, 14½″ × 13½″

This quilt design uses multiple sizes of blocks with added frames and sashing.
It's the perfect choice for tablecloths that have a variety of motif sizes.

FABRIC REQUIREMENTS

Based on 42″ fabric width.

Tablecloth motifs: 4 rectangles 12″ × 14″ (A1)
and 2 rectangles 14½″ × 13½″ (A2) for blocks

Print: 3 squares 7½″ × 7½″ for fussy-cut blocks (A3)

(We used small motifs from the tablecloth.)

Gray 1: 1⅜ yards for block frames and binding

Gray 2: 1⅛ yards for center block corners,
center block frame, sashing squares,
vertical sashing, and border corners

Gray 3: ½ yard for center block
frame and sashing squares

Gray 4: 2⅛ yards for sashing squares and
lengthwise-cut outer border (1½ yards for sashing
squares and crosswise-cut and pieced border)

Coral 1: ¾ yard for center block corners, center block
frame, vertical sashing, and pieced sashing centers

Coral 2: ¾ yard for pieced sashing centers and corners,
sashing squares, inner border, and border centers

Coral 3: ¼ yard for pieced sashing
blocks and sashing squares

Coral 4: ¼ yard for pieced sashing
blocks and sashing squares

Coral 5: ⅓ yard for pieced sashing
blocks and sashing squares

NOTE *Our small center-diamond sashing
blocks were made using a variety of fabrics,
scrappy style. The following cutting and piecing
instructions use a more repetitive style to
simplify things.*

CUTTING

Gray 1

Cut 7 strips 2¾″ × fabric width; subcut into:
    8 strips 2¾″ × 14″ (B) and
    8 strips 2¾″ × 16½″ (C).

Cut 4 strips 1½″ × fabric width; subcut into:
    4 strips 1½″ × 13½″ (D) and
    4 strips 1½″ × 16½″ (E).

Cut 8 strips 2¼″ × fabric width for the binding.

Gray 2

Cut 2 strips 4½″ × fabric width; subcut into:
    4 strips 4½″ × 16½″ (H).

Cut 1 strip 6½″ × fabric width; subcut into:
    2 squares 6½″ × 6½″, and then cut in half
    diagonally (I).

Cut 1 strip 3½″ × fabric width; subcut into:
    2 strips 3½″ × 10½″ (J).

Cut 2 strips 4½″ × fabric width; subcut into:
    4 strips 4½″ × 18½″ (L).

Cut 1 strip 4½″ × fabric width; subcut into:
    8 squares 4½″ × 4½″ for sashing squares.

Cut 1 strip 2½″ × fabric width; subcut into:
    16 squares 2½″ × 2½″ (S).

Gray 3

Cut 1 strip 3″ × fabric width; subcut into:
    2 strips 3″ × 16½″ (K).

Cut 2 strips 4½″ × fabric width; subcut into:
    16 squares 4½″ × 4½″ for sashing squares.

Gray 4

Cut the border strips first on the lengthwise grain.

Cut 2 lengthwise strips 4½″ × 69½″ (X).

Cut 2 lengthwise strips 4½″ × 58½″ (Y).

Cut 4 strips 4½″ × remaining fabric width; subcut into:
    16 squares 4½″ × 4½″ for sashing squares.

Coral 1

Cut 1 strip 6½″ × fabric width; subcut into:
    4 squares 6½″ × 6½″, and then cut in half
    diagonally (F).

Cut 1 strip 3½″ × fabric width; subcut into:
    4 strips 3½″ × 10½″ (G).

Cut 1 strip 4½″ × fabric width; subcut into:
    2 strips 4½″ × 15½″ (M).

Cut 1 strip 4½″ × fabric width; subcut into:
    4 squares 4½″ × 4½″ (T).

Coral 2

Cut 1 strip 2½″ × fabric width; subcut into:
    16 squares 2½″ × 2½″ (P).

Cut 1 strip 4½″ × fabric width; subcut into:
    4 squares 4½″ × 4½″ (R).

Cut 7 strips 1½″ × fabric width; sew together
into a continuous strip and subcut into:
    2 strips 1½″ × 67½″ (V) and
    2 strips 1½″ × 58½″ (W).

Coral 3

Cut 1 strip 2½″ × fabric width; subcut into:
    16 squares 2½″ × 2½″ (Q).

Coral 4

Cut 1 strip 4½″ × fabric width; subcut into:
    4 squares 4½″ × 4½″ (N).

Coral 5

Cut 1 strip 4½″ × fabric width; subcut into:
    4 squares 4½″ × 4½″ (O).

Cut 1 strip 4½″ × fabric width; subcut into:
    4 squares 4½″ × 4½″ (U).

Blocks

Use ¼″ seam allowances.

Blocks for Side Sections

1. Sew a B strip to each side of an A1 rectangle. Press.

2. Sew C strips to the top and bottom of A1. Press. Make 4.

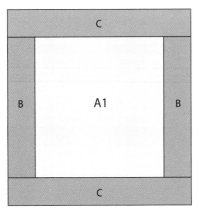

Block A1; make 4.

3. Sew a D strip to each side of an A2 rectangle. Press.

4. Sew E strips to the top and bottom of A2. Press. Make 2.

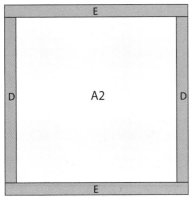

Block A2; make 2.

Blocks for Center Section

1. Sew F triangles to two opposite sides of an A3 square. Press.

2. Sew F triangles to the remaining sides of A3. Press.

3. Trim to 10½″ × 10½″, making sure the block is centered and symmetrical.

4. Sew G strips to the sides of the block. Press.

5. Sew H strips to the top and bottom of the block. Press. Make 2.

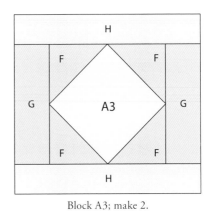

Block A3; make 2.

6. Sew I triangles to two opposite sides of the remaining A3 square. Press.

7. Sew I triangles to the remaining sides of A3. Press.

8. Trim to 10½″ × 10½″, making sure the block is centered and symmetrical.

9. Sew J strips to the sides of the block. Press.

10. Sew K strips to the top and bottom of the block. Press.

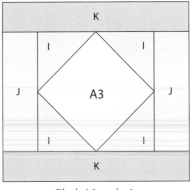

Block A3; make 1.

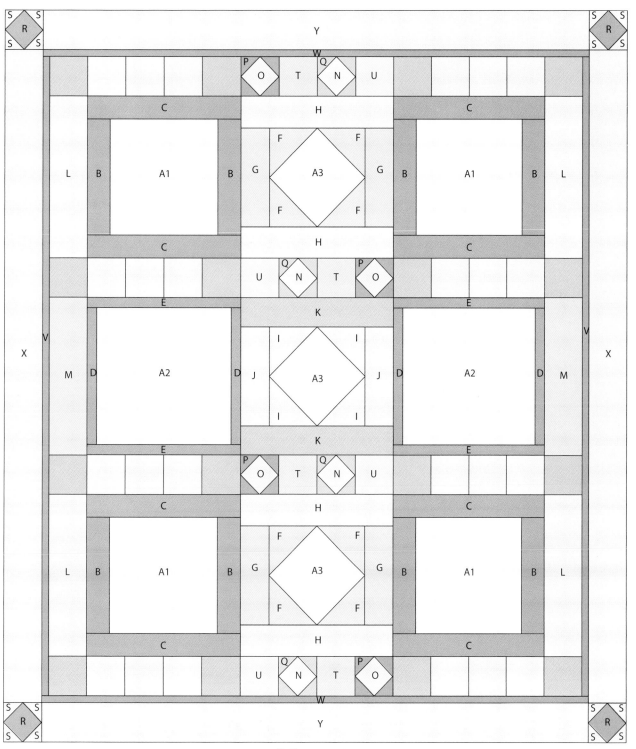

Quilt construction

Construction

1. Lay out the blocks.

2. Sew the blocks together in 3 horizontal rows. Press.

3. Sew L strips to the ends of Rows 1 and 3. Press.

4. Sew an M strip to each end of Row 2. Press.

Horizontal-Sashing Squares

1. Sew 5 of the 4½″ × 4½″ gray sashing squares together, as shown. Make 8.

Gray 3	Gray 4	Gray 2	Gray 4	Gray 3

Gray sashing square units; make 8.

2. Mark the P squares with a diagonal line from corner to corner.

3. Align one of these marked squares on a corner of an O square. Sew on the marked line and trim ¼″ outside the sewn line. Press.

Mark diagonal line, align corners, and stitch as shown.

4. Repeat Step 3 to add a P square to the opposite corner of the O square.

Add P squares to opposite corners of O.

5. Add the remaining P squares to the O square. Press. Make 4 blocks.

Add remaining P squares. Make 4.

6. Repeat Steps 3–5 to add Q to N and S to R.

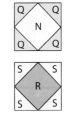

Make 4 N/Q blocks and 4 R/S blocks.

7. Sew the sashing squares together as follows:

U to N/Q to T to O/P. Make 4.

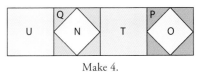

Make 4.

8. Sew the gray sashing strip sets to the peach sashing, referring to the quilt construction diagram.

9. Sew the sashing strips to the rows of blocks.

Borders

1. Sew V strips to the sides of the quilt top. Press.

2. Add W strips to the top and bottom of the quilt top. Press.

3. Sew X strips to the sides of the quilt top. Press.

4. Add the R/S blocks to the ends of the 2 Y strips. Press.

5. Add the R/S/Y units to the top and bottom of the quilt top. Press.

Finishing

Layer, baste, quilt, bind, and label your quilt.

Rosesprays

Designed and pieced by Rose Sheifer, quilted by Darla Padilla and Jocelyn Marzan

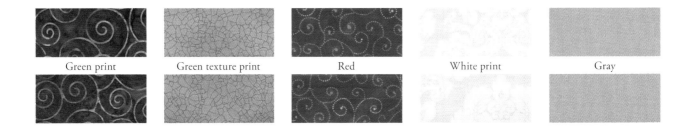

Green print | Green texture print | Red | White print | Gray

Finished size: 77½″ × 89½″ | **Block size (unfinished):** 17½″ × 17½″

Tablecloth motif size (cut): 15½″ × 15½″

Make this sophisticated quilt using only five tablecloth motifs. Add dimension with prairie points and button embellishments.

Because of permanent stains, this tablecloth had only five usable flower-spray motifs to incorporate into the quilt. For the background I chose a soft gray Victorian print that resembles wallpaper. Bright red and jade green were used to complement the tablecloth colors. This quilt has an elegant vintage look.

FABRIC REQUIREMENTS

Based on 42″ fabric width.

Tablecloth motifs: 5 motifs 15½″ × 15½″ for blocks (A)

Green print: ½ yard for block frames

Green texture print: 1 yard for prairie points

Red: ⅝ yard for small blocks and inner border

White print: 4⅝ yards for small blocks and quilt background

Gray: 1⅛ yards for background strips, outer border, and binding

Backing: 82″ × 94″

Batting: 82″ × 94″

1″ buttons (optional): 16

CUTTING

Green print

Cut 10 strips 1½″ × fabric width; subcut into:
    10 strips 1½″ × 15½″ (B) and
    10 strips 1½″ × 17½″ (C).

Green texture print

Cut 4 strips 8″ by fabric width; subcut into:
    20 squares 8″ × 8″ (D).

Red

Cut 8 strips 1½″ × fabric width; piece into
1 continuous strip and subcut into:
    2 strips 1½″ × 81½″ (P) and
    2 strips 1½″ × 71½″ (Q).

Cut a strip 5½″ × fabric width; subcut into:
    4 squares 5½″ × 5½″ (E).

White print

Cut 1 strip 4¾″ × fabric width; subcut into:
    8 squares 4¾″ × 4¾″, and then cut in half
    diagonally (F).

Cut 12 strips 9½″ × fabric width; subcut into:
    4 strips 9½″ × 28½″ (N).
    Trim and subcut remaining strips into:
    4 strips 8½″ × 29½″ (G) and
    4 strips 8½″ × 23½″ (I).

Cut 2 strips 9½″ × fabric width; subcut into:
    4 strips 9½″ × 17½″ (K).

Cut 2 strips 9½″ × fabric width; subcut into:
    4 strips 9½″ × 13½″ (L).

Cut 1 strip 2½″ × fabric width; subcut into:
    2 strips 2½″ × 7½″ (O) and
    4 strips 2½″ × 3½″ (T).

Gray

Cut 8 strips 3½″ × fabric width; piece
into 4 long strips, and subcut into:
    2 strips 3½″ × 83½″ (R) and
    2 strips 3½″ × 77½″ (S).

Cut 4 strips 1½″ × fabric width; subcut into:
    2 strips 1½″ × 29½″ (H),
    2 strips 1½″ × 23½″ (J),
    4 strips 1½″ × 9½″ (M), and
    2 strips 1½″ × 2½″ (U).

Blocks

Use ¼" seam allowances.

Large Blocks

1. Sew a B strip to each side of an A square. Press.

2. Sew C strips to the top and bottom edges of A. Press.

3. Repeat to make 5 large blocks.

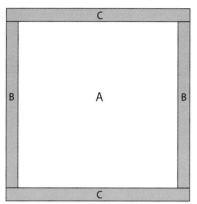

Sew frame strips to block.

4. Fold the prairie points (D) as shown. Press.

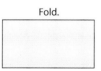

Start with square.

Fold square in half and press.

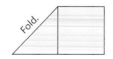

Fold down upper left corner and press.

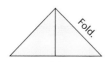

Fold down upper right corner and press.

5. Center and baste the prairie points in position around the framed A blocks.

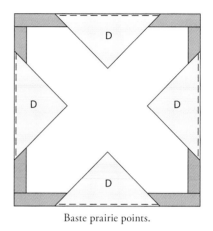

Baste prairie points.

Small Blocks

1. Sew an F triangle, centered, to opposite corners of an E square. Press.

2. Repeat Step 1 to add the other F triangles to the E square. Press. Make 4.

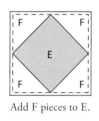

Add F pieces to E.

3. Trim these blocks to 7½" × 7½", making sure the blocks are centered and symmetrical.

Background

1. Sew an H strip between 2 G strips. Press. Make 2.

2. Sew a J strip between 2 I strips. Press. Make 2.

3. Sew an M strip between a K and an L strip. Press. Make 4.

4. Sew a U strip between 2 T strips. Make 2.

Construction

1. Lay out the pieces, referring to the quilt construction diagram.

2. Sew the large tablecloth blocks and background units together in 3 columns, making sure to stitch the prairie points into the seams. Press.

3. Sew these columns together, making sure to stitch the prairie points into the seams. Press.

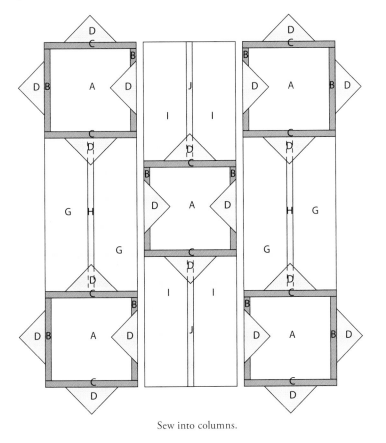

Sew into columns.

4. Sew an O strip to one side of a small block. Press. Make 2.

5. Sew N strips to the top and bottom of the small block / O unit to make the vertical side sections, noting the position of the O strip. Press. Make 2.

6. Add these units to the sides of the quilt top, with the O strips facing out. Press.

7. Sew T/U/T to one side of a small block. Press. Make 2.

8. Sew this small block unit to the L side of 2 K/L units, following the quilt construction diagram and noting the position of the T/U/T unit. Press. Make 2.

9. Add these units to the top and bottom of the quilt top. Press.

Borders

Inner Border

1. Sew a P strip to each side of the quilt top. Press.

2. Sew Q strips to the top and bottom edges of the quilt top. Press.

Outer Border

1. Sew an R strip to each side of the quilt top. Press.

2. Sew S strips to the top and bottom edges of the quilt top. Press.

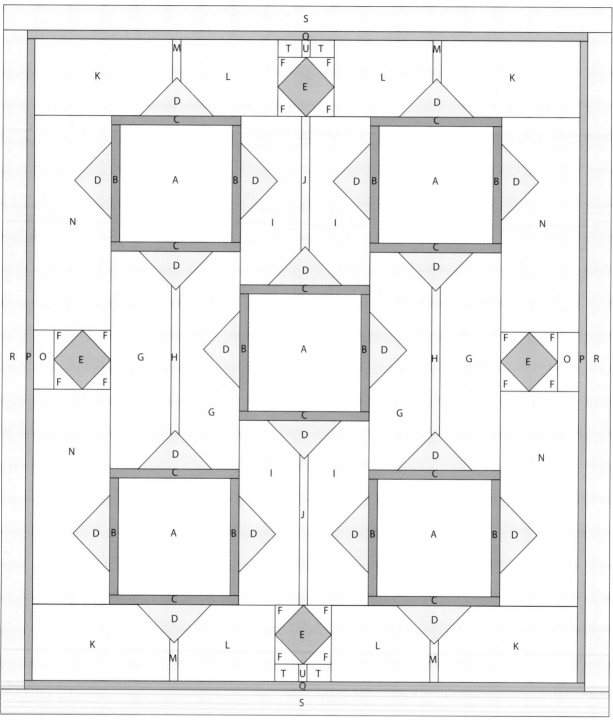

Quilt construction

Finishing

Layer, baste, quilt, bind, and label your quilt. Embellish with buttons on the corners
of the small block centers and hand stitch to tack down the corners of the prairie points.

Vintage Roses

Designed, pieced, and appliquéd by Rose Sheifer, quilted by Liz Aneloski

Green   Yellow   Blue   Print   Dark blue

Finished size: 44½″ × 44½″ | **Block size (unfinished):** 15½″ × 15½″

Tablecloth motif size (cut): 13½″ × 13½″

To make this vintage tablecloth quilt, I cut out and appliquéd seven of the blue roses. The center square was in perfect condition, so it could be used in its entirety. Surrounding the elements with reproduction vintage fabric and fresh colors pulled it all together.

FABRIC REQUIREMENTS

Based on 42″ fabric width.

Tablecloth motif: 1 center square 14½″ × 14½″ (trimmed to 13½″ × 13½″ after appliqué) (A)

Green: ½ yard for center-block frame, inner border, and pieced outer border

Yellow: 1 yard for prairie points, appliqué blocks, and pieced outer border

Blue: ⅝ yard for background and pieced outer border

Flowers: 7 appliqué motifs for center and border bocks (We were able to fussy cut the flowers from the tablecloth.)

Print: ¾ yard for middle border

Dark blue: ½ yard for binding

Backing: 49″ × 49″

Batting: 49″ × 49″

4 buttons (optional): 1″ diameter

CUTTING

Green

Cut 2 strips 1½″ × fabric width; subcut into:
2 strips 1½″ × 13½″ (B) and
2 strips 1½″ × 15½″ (C).

Cut 4 strips 1½″ × fabric width; subcut into:
2 strips 1½″ × 25½″ (G) and
2 strips 1½″ × 27½″ (H).

Cut 1 strip 6″ × fabric width; subcut into:
10 strips 3″ × 6″ (M).

Yellow

Cut 1 strip 8½″ × fabric width; subcut into:
4 squares 8½″ × 8½″ (D).

Cut 2 strips 7½″ × fabric width; subcut into:
6 squares 7½″ × 7½″ (trimmed to 6½″ × 6½″ after appliqué) (I).

Cut 1 strip 6″ × fabric width; subcut into:
10 strips 3″ × 6″ (N).

Blue

Cut the 2 longest strips first.

Cut 2 strips 5½″ × fabric width; subcut into:
2 strips 5½″ × 25½″ (F) and
2 strips 5½″ × 15½″ (E).

Cut 2 strips 3″ × fabric width; subcut into:
6 strips 3″ × 6″ (L1) and
4 strips 3″ × 6¼″ (L2).

Print

Cut the 2 longest strips first.

Cut 3 strips 6½″ × fabric width; subcut into:
2 strips 6½″ × 27½″ (J) and
4 strips 6½″ × 11″ (K).

Dark blue

Cut 5 strips 2¼″ × fabric width for the binding.

Blocks

Use ¼″ seam allowances.

Center Block

1. Appliqué a flower in the center of the A square. Trim A to 13½″ × 13½″, making sure the flower is centered and the block is symmetrical.

2. Sew a B strip to each side of A. Press.

3. Sew C strips to the top and bottom edges of A. Press.

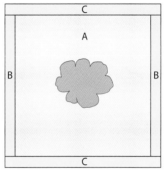

Sew frame strips to block.

4. Fold the prairie points (D) as shown. Press.

Start with a square.

Fold square in half and press.

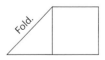

Fold down upper left corner and press.

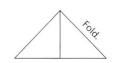

Fold down upper right corner and press.

5. Center and baste the prairie points in position.

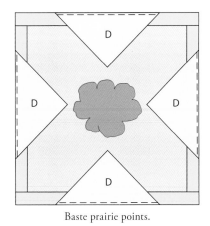

Baste prairie points.

6. Sew an E strip to each side of the block; be sure the prairie points are sewn into the seam. Press.

7. Sew F strips to the top and bottom edges of the block; be sure the prairie points are sewn into the seam. Press.

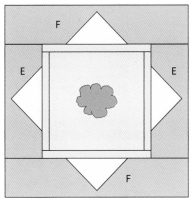

Add E and F, sewing prairie points into seam.

Borders

Inner Borders

1. Sew a G strip to each side of the quilt top. Press.

2. Sew H strips to the top and bottom edges of the quilt top. Press.

Middle Appliquéd Borders

1. Appliqué the flowers to the I squares. Trim each square to 6½″ × 6½″, making sure the block is centered and symmetrical. Make 6.

2. Sew an I square between 2 K rectangles. Press. Make 2.

3. Sew an I square to each end of a J rectangle. Press. Make 2.

4. Sew the side appliquéd borders on first, press, and then add the top and bottom appliquéd borders. Press.

Outer Pieced Borders

1. Make 2 side outer borders by sewing outer border pieces together along the short edges in the following order: L2 / M / N / L1 / M / N / L2. Press.

2. Sew the side borders to the quilt top. Press.

3. Make the 2 remaining outer borders by sewing the remaining outer border pieces together along the short edges in the following order: M / N / L1 / M / N / L1 / M / N.

4. Sew the top and bottom pieced outer borders to the quilt top. Press.

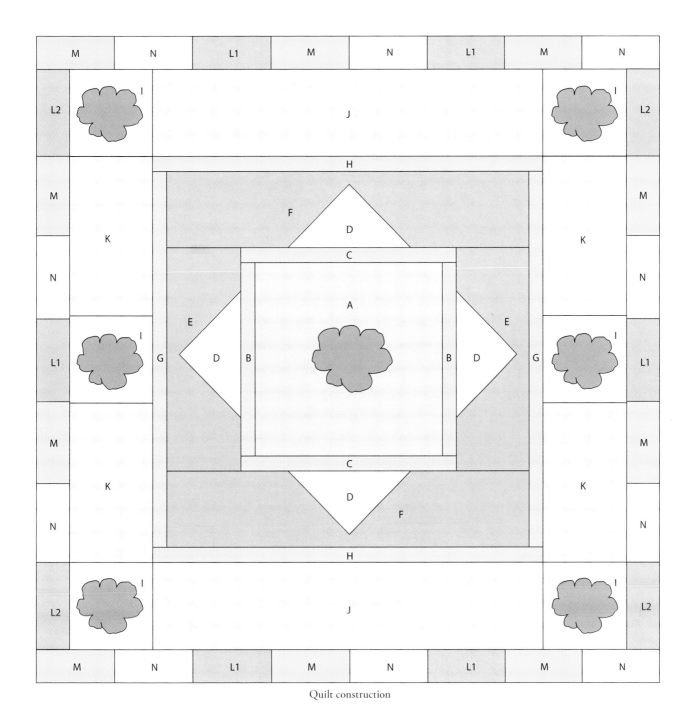

Quilt construction

Finishing

Layer, baste, quilt, bind, and label your quilt. Embellish with buttons
to tack down the corners of the prairie points (see photo, page 77).

Blue Roses

Designed and pieced by Rose Sheifer, quilted by Darla Padilla

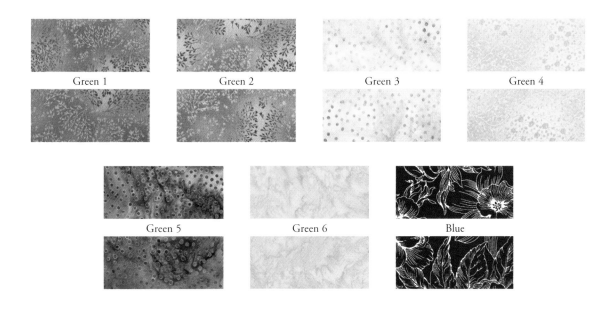

Green 1 Green 2 Green 3 Green 4

Green 5 Green 6 Blue

Finished size: 60½″ × 90½″ | **Block size (unfinished):** 12½″ × 22½″, 14½″ × 20½″, 12½″ × 15½″

Tablecloth motif sizes (cut): 10½″ × 20½″, 12½″ × 18½″, 10½″ × 13½″

This quilt design uses three sizes of blocks with added frames. It's the perfect choice for tablecloths that have a variety of motif sizes.

FABRIC REQUIREMENTS

Based on 42″ fabric width.

Tablecloth motifs: 10 pieces total:

  2 rectangles 10½″ × 20½″ (A1)

  2 rectangles 12½″ × 18½″ (A2)

  2 rectangles 10½″ × 20½″ (A3)

  2 rectangles 10½″ × 13½″ (A4)

  2 rectangles 10½″ × 20½″ (A5)

Green 1: ⅜ yard for vertical strips and border

Green 2: ½ yard for block frames, vertical strips, and border

Green 3: ¾ yard for block frames, vertical strips, and border

Green 4: ⅝ yard for block frames, vertical strips, and border

Green 5: ⅝ yard for block frames, vertical strips, and border

Green 6: ½ yard for vertical strips and border

Blue: 2¼ yards for background and binding

Backing: 65″ × 95″

Batting: 65″ × 95″

CUTTING

Green 1

Cut 2 strips 2″ × fabric width: subcut into:
  4 strips 2″ × 14½″ (Q).

Green 2

Cut 4 strips 1½″ × fabric width; subcut into:
  4 strips 1½″ × 18½″ (D) and
  4 strips 1½″ × 14½″ (E).

Green 3

Cut 7 strips 1½″ × fabric width; subcut into:
  4 strips 1½″ × 20½″ (B),
  4 strips 1½″ × 12½″ (C),
  4 strips 1½″ × 20½″ (F), and
  4 strips 1½″ × 12½″ (G).

Cut 2 strips 2″ × fabric width: subcut into:
  4 strips 2″ × 14½″ (Q).

Green 4

Cut 3 strips 1½″ × fabric width; subcut into:
  4 strips 1½″ × 13½″ (H) and
  4 strips 1½″ × 12½″ (I).

Cut 2 strips 2″ × fabric width: subcut into:
  4 strips 2″ × 14½″ (Q).

Green 5

Cut 4 strips 1½″ × fabric width; subcut into:
  4 strips 1½″ × 20½″ (J) and
  4 strips 1½″ × 12½″ (K).

Cut 2 strips 2″ × fabric width; subcut into:
  4 strips 2″ × 14½″ (Q).

Green 6

Cut 4 strips 2″ × fabric width; subcut into:
  8 strips 2″ × 14½″ (Q).

Assorted Greens (1–6)

Cut 10 strips 3⅞″ × fabric width; subcut into:
  96 squares 3⅞″ × 3⅞″, and then cut in half
  diagonally for the border blocks.

Blue

Cut 12 strips 2½″ × fabric width; subcut into:
  12 strips 2½″ × 22½″ (L) and
  5 strips 2½″ × 16½″ (P).

From the leftover 2½″ strips, trim and subcut into:
  4 strips 2½″ × 15½″ (N).

Cut 2 strips 1½″ × fabric width; subcut into:
  4 strips 1½″ × 20½″ (M).

Cut 4 strips 5½″ × fabric width; subcut into:
  8 strips 5½″ × 16½″ (O).

Cut 8 strips 2¼″ × fabric width for the binding.

Blocks

Use ¼″ seam allowances.

Blocks for Side Sections

1. Sew a B strip to each side of an A1 rectangle. Press.

2. Sew C strips to the top and bottom of A1. Press.

3. Sew an L strip to each side of the block. Press. Make 2.

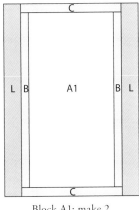

Block A1; make 2.

4. Sew a D strip to each side of an A2 rectangle. Press.

5. Sew E strips to the top and bottom of A2. Press.

6. Sew an M strip to each side of the block. Press. Make 2.

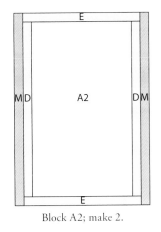

Block A2; make 2.

7. Sew an F strip to each side of an A3 rectangle. Press.

8. Sew G strips to the top and bottom of A3. Press.

9. Sew an L strip to each side of the block. Press. Make 2.

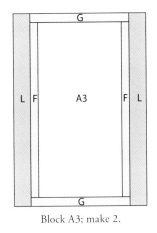

Block A3; make 2.

Blocks for Center Section

1. Sew an H strip to each side of an A4 rectangle. Press.

2. Sew I strips to the top and bottom of A4. Press.

3. Sew an N strip to each side of the block. Press. Make 2.

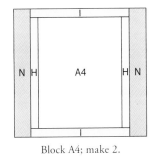

Block A4; make 2.

4. Sew a strip J to each side of an A5 rectangle. Press.

5. Sew K strips to the top and bottom of A5. Press.

6. Sew an L strip to each side of the block. Press. Make 2.

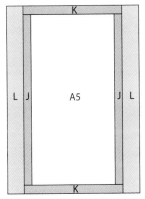

Block A5; make 2.

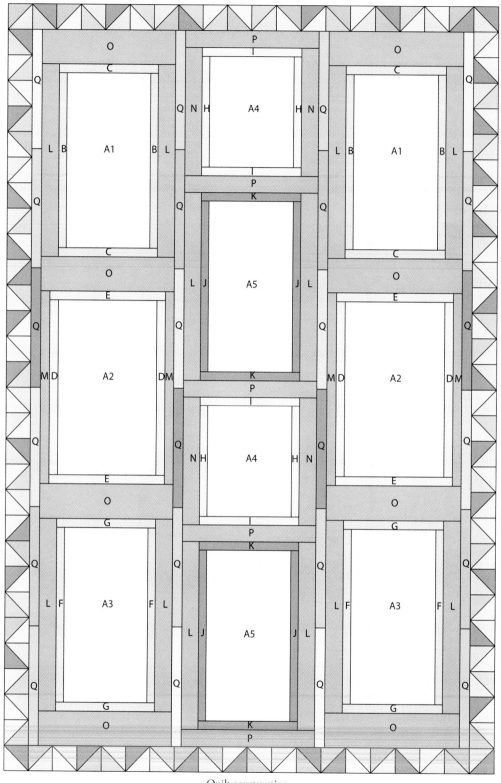

Quilt construction

Construction

1. Lay out the blocks and background.

2. Sew one set of side section blocks together in columns, with O strips on the top, bottom, and between the blocks. Press. Repeat to make the other side section.

3. Sew the center section blocks together in a column, with P strips on the top, bottom, and between the blocks. Press.

4. Sew the Q strips into 4 long strips of 6 pieces each, referring to the photo for color placement.

5. Sew the columns together with the Q strips on each side and between the sections. Press.

Borders

1. Sew the border-block triangles together in pairs along the diagonal sides. Press. Make 96.

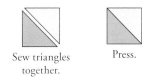

Sew triangles together.　　Press.

2. Sew 28 of the border blocks together in random order, alternating the direction, and add this strip to one side of the quilt top. Press. Repeat for the other side.

3. Sew 20 of the border blocks together in random order, alternating the direction, and add this strip to the top edge of the quilt top. Press. Repeat for the bottom border.

Finishing

Layer, baste, quilt, bind, and label your quilt.

Delicate Daisies

Designed and pieced by Rose Sheifer, quilted by Darla Padilla

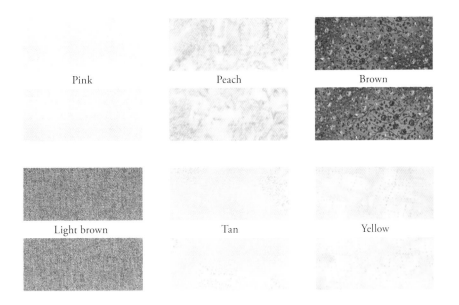

Pink Peach Brown

Light brown Tan Yellow

Finished size: 78½″ × 80½″ | **Block size (unfinished):** 16½″ × 16½″
Tablecloth motif size (cut): 11½″ × 11½″

Fussy cut the small blocks from a coordinating print fabric or from the print of the tablecloth.

FABRIC REQUIREMENTS

Based on 42″ fabric width.

Tablecloth motifs: 8 squares 11½″ × 11½″ for blocks (A)

Pink: ⅔ yard for block frames

Peach: ⅔ yard for block frames

Print: at least ⅛ yard, or enough to fussy cut 9 motifs for center and border blocks (We were able to fussy cut the daisies from the tablecloth.)

Brown: 2¼ yards for center block frame and outer border

Light brown: 2⅝ yards for background and binding

Tan: ⅝ yard for inner border

Yellow: ⅓ yard for border block frames

Backing: 83″ × 85″

Batting: 83″ × 85″

CUTTING

Pink
Cut 7 strips 3″ × fabric
width; subcut into:
    8 strips 3″ × 11½″ (B) and
    8 strips 3″ × 16½″ (D).

Peach
Cut 7 strips 3″ × fabric
width; subcut into:
    8 strips 3″ × 11½″ (C) and
    8 strips 3″ × 16½″ (E).

Print
Cut 1 square 4½″ × 4½″ (F).

Cut 8 squares 4½″ × 4½″ (N).

Brown

Cut 1 strip 3″ × fabric width; subcut into:
  2 strips 3″ × 4½″ (G) and
  2 strips 3″ × 9½″ (H).

Cut 6 strips 1″ × fabric width; subcut into:
  16 strips 1″ × 6½″ (Q) and
  16 strips 1″ × 7½″ (R).

Cut 8 strips 7½″ × fabric width; subcut into:
  4 strips 7½″ × 30″ (S) and
  4 strips 7½″ × 29″ (T).

Light brown

Cut 4 squares 13″ × 13″, and then cut
each in half diagonally (I).

Cut 1 strip 7½″ × fabric width; subcut into:
  2 rectangles 7½″ × 9½″ (J).

Cut 2 strips 4″ × fabric width; trim to:
  2 strips 4″ × 23½″ (K).

Cut 3 strips 3″ × fabric width; sew into a continuous strip, and then subcut into:
  2 strips 3″ × 62½″ (L).

Cut 2 strips 7½″ × fabric width; subcut into:
  4 rectangles 7½″ × 16½″ (M).

Cut 9 strips 2¼″ × fabric width for the binding.

Tan

Cut 7 strips 2½″ × fabric width; sew into
a continuous strip and subcut into:
  2 strips 2½″ × 62½″ (U) and
  2 strips 2½″ × 64½″ (V).

Yellow

Cut 5 strips 1½″ × fabric width; subcut into:
  16 strips 1½″ × 4½″ (O) and
  16 strips 1½″ × 6½″ (P).

Blocks

Use ¼″ seam allowances.

Main Blocks

Please note that our blocks were made by randomly piecing them scrappy style. The instructions and quilt construction diagram below use a more repetitive style to simplify the process.

1. Sew a B strip to the left side of an A square. Press.

2. Sew a C strip to the right side of A. Press.

3. Sew a D strip to the top edge of A. Press.

4. Sew an E strip to the bottom edge of A. Press.

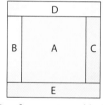

Sew frame strips to block.

5. Repeat Steps 1–4 to make 8 blocks.

6. On 2 of the blocks, sew an I triangle to a side, centering the triangle on the block. Press.

7. Add another I triangle to the opposite side of the block. Press.

8. Add the other 2 I triangles to the remaining sides. Press.

9. Trim the block to 23½″ × 23½″, making sure the block is centered and symmetrical.

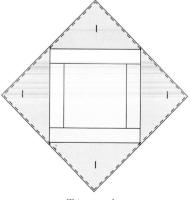

Trim evenly.

Center Block

1. Sew a G strip to each side of the F square. Press.

2. Sew H strips to the top and bottom edges of F. Press.

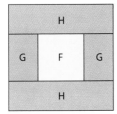

Sew frame strips to block.

3. Sew a J rectangle to each H/G/H side of the block. Press.

4. Sew K strips to the top and bottom edges of the block. Press.

Construction

1. Lay out the blocks and background pieces.

2. Sew M rectangles between the blocks in the side sections.

3. Sew the blocks together in columns. Press.

4. Sew the columns together with L strips between the columns. Press.

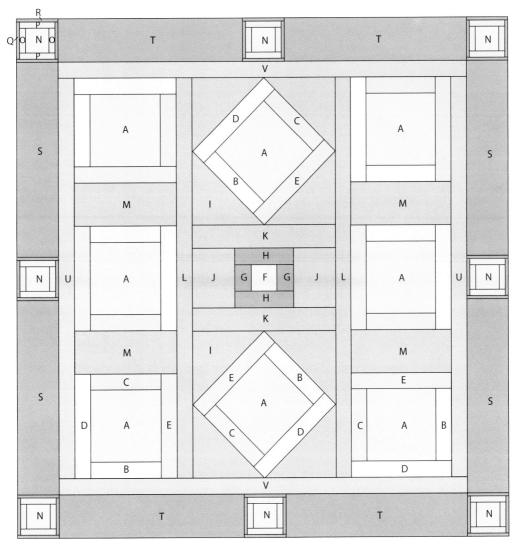

Quilt construction

Borders

Inner Borders

1. Add a U strip to each side of the quilt top. Press.

2. Add V strips to the top and bottom edges of the quilt top. Press.

Outer Border Blocks

1. Sew an O strip to each side of an N square. Press.

2. Sew P strips to the top and bottom edges of N. Press.

3. Sew a Q strip to each side of the block. Press.

4. Sew R strips to the top and bottom of the block. Press. Make 8.

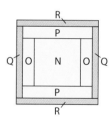

Sew frame strips to blocks.

Border Construction

Construct and add the borders as shown in the quilt construction diagram (page 91). Add the side borders first and then the top and bottom borders.

Finishing

Layer, baste, quilt, bind, and label your quilt.

Appendix

Seam Allowances

A ¼" seam allowance is used for most projects. It's a good idea to do a test seam before you begin sewing to check that your ¼" is accurate. Accuracy is the key to successful piecing.

There is no need to backstitch. Seamlines will be crossed by other seams, which will anchor them.

Pressing

In general, press seams toward the darker fabric. Press lightly in an up-and-down motion. Avoid using a very hot iron or overironing, which can distort the shapes and blocks. Be especially careful when pressing bias edges as they stretch easily.

Binding

Trim excess batting and backing even with the edges of the quilt top.

Double-Fold Straight-Grain Binding

1. If you want a ¼" finished binding, cut the binding strips 2¼" wide and piece them together with diagonal seams to make a continuous binding strip.

2. Trim the seam allowances to ¼". Press the seams open.

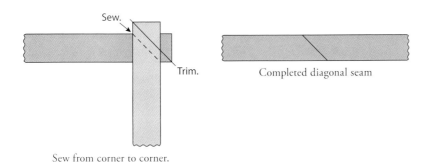

Sew from corner to corner.

3. Press the entire strip in half lengthwise with wrong sides together.

4. With raw edges even, pin the binding to the front edge of the quilt a few inches away from a corner, leaving the first few inches of the binding unattached. Start sewing, using a ¼" seam allowance.

5. Stop ¼" from the first corner and backstitch one stitch.

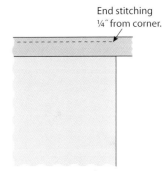

Stitch to ¼" from corner.

Lift the presser foot and needle. Rotate the quilt one-quarter turn to the left.

Fold the binding at a right angle, so it extends straight above the quilt and the fold forms a 45° angle in the corner.

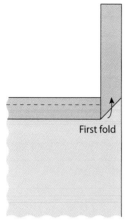

First fold for miter

Then bring the binding strip down even with the edge of the quilt. Begin sewing at the folded edge. Repeat in the same manner at all the corners.

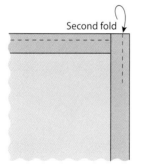

Second fold alignment

6. Continue stitching until you are back near the beginning of the binding strip.

Finishing the Binding Ends
Method 1

After stitching around the quilt, open the beginning tail of the binding and fold ¼″ to the wrong side of the fabric. Refold the binding in half lengthwise. Place the end tail of the binding strip into the beginning folded end. Finish attaching the binding, stitching slightly beyond the starting stitches. Trim off the excess binding. Fold the binding to the back of the quilt and hand stitch, mitering the corners.

Method 2

For extra help, see C&T Publishing's website at www .ctpub.com. Click on "Resources" at the top of the page, and then click on "Quiltmaking Basics: Tips & Techniques for Quiltmaking & More." Click on "Completing a Binding with an Invisible Seam" under "Quilting Tips."

1. Fold the ending tail of the binding back on itself where it meets the beginning binding tail. From the fold, measure and mark the cut width of the binding strip. Cut the ending binding tail to this measurement. For example, if the binding is cut 2¼″ wide, measure from the fold on the ending tail of the binding 2¼″ and cut the binding tail to this length.

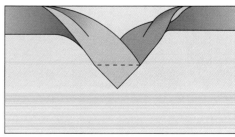

Cut binding tail.

2. Open both tails. Place one tail on top of the other tail at a right angle, with right sides together. Mark a diagonal line from corner to corner and stitch on the line. Check that you've done it correctly and that the binding fits the quilt; then trim the seam allowance to ¼″. Press open.

Stitch ends of binding diagonally.

3. Refold the binding and stitch this binding section in place on the quilt. Fold the binding to the back of the quilt and hand stitch.

About the Authors

Rose Sheifer grew up on the East Coast, where her passion for creativity began at an early age. Her family sewed clothing for wholesale distributors in the Garment District of New York City. Everyone in her family  learned to sew and worked in the factory, like it or not.

She earned her Bachelor of Arts in illustration at Moore College of Art in Philadelphia. This led to a career in publishing, as a production specialist and freelance graphic designer for nationwide publishers, as well as a career as a fine-arts muralist.

After designing more than 100 quilt books, she felt it was time to put her design skills together with fabric. That, combined with her collection of vintage linens and glassware, spurred the idea for *Vintage Tablecloth Quilts*.

Rose resides in the San Francisco Bay Area with her husband and son. She is now fully addicted to fabric!

Liz Aneloski learned to quilt in the 1980s when her daughters were very young. She has been an editor at C&T Publishing for a couple of decades, authored eight books, nurtured her marriage for 30 years (and counting), and  watched her girls become amazing married women. She says, "What more could a person ask for?"

Liz lives in California with her husband and Toby, a 14-pound four-legged ball of energy with a tail that never stops wagging.

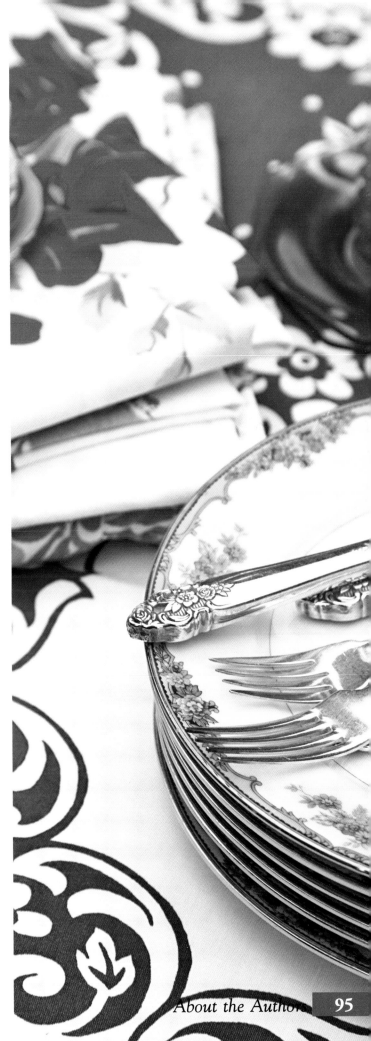

Great Titles *from* C&T PUBLISHING & STASH BOOKS

Available at your local retailer or **www.ctpub.com** *or* **800-284-1114**

For a list of other fine books from C&T Publishing, visit our website to view our catalog online.

C&T PUBLISHING, INC.
P.O. Box 1456
Lafayette, CA 94549
800-284-1114

Email: ctinfo@ctpub.com
Website: www.ctpub.com

C&T Publishing's professional photography services are now available to the public. Visit us at www.ctmediaservices.com.

Tips and Techniques can be found at www.ctpub.com > Consumer Resources > Quiltmaking Basics: Tips & Techniques for Quiltmaking & More

For quilting supplies:

COTTON PATCH
1025 Brown Ave.
Lafayette, CA 94549
Store: 925-284-1177
Mail order: 925-283-7883

Email: CottonPa@aol.com
Website: www.quiltusa.com

Note: Fabrics shown may not be currently available, as fabric manufacturers keep most fabrics in print for only a short time.